P9-DNF-005

A Brief History of Happiness

To C. C.

a brief history of happiness

Nicholas White

Blackwell
Publishing

© 2006 by Nicholas White

BLACKWELL PUBLISHING
350 Main Street, Malden, MA 02148-5020, USA
9600 Garsington Road, Oxford OX4 2DQ, UK
550 Swanston Street, Carlton, Victoria 3053, Australia

The right of Nicholas White to be identified as the Author of this
Work has been asserted in accordance with the UK Copyright,
Designs, and Patents Act 1988.

All rights reserved. No part of this publication may be reproduced,
stored in a retrieval system, or transmitted, in any form or by any means,
electronic, mechanical, photocopying, recording or otherwise,
except as permitted by the UK Copyright, Designs, and Patents Act 1988,
without the prior permission of the publisher.

First published 2006 by Blackwell Publishing Ltd

3   2007

Library of Congress Cataloging-in-Publication Data

White, Nicholas P., 1942–
A brief history of happiness / Nicholas White.
p. cm.
Includes bibliographical references and index.
ISBN-13: 978-1-4051-1519-3 (hardback : alk. paper)
ISBN-10: 1-4051-1519-X (hardback : alk. paper)
ISBN-13: 978-1-4051-1520-9 (pbk. : alk. paper)
ISBN-10: 1-4051-1520-3 (pbk. : alk. paper)   1. Happiness—History.
I. Title.
BJ1481.W65 2006
170—dc22

2005024028

A catalogue record for this title is available from the British Library.

Set in 10.5/14pt Minion
by Graphicraft Limited, Hong Kong
Printed and bound in the United Kingdom
by TJ International, Padstow, Cornwall

The publisher's policy is to use permanent paper from mills that operate
a sustainable forestry policy, and which has been manufactured from pulp
processed using acid-free and elementary chlorine-free practices.
Furthermore, the publisher ensures that the text paper and cover board
used have met acceptable environmental accreditation standards.

For further information on
Blackwell Publishing, visit our website:
www.blackwellpublishing.com

Contents

Preface

> Now anticipation is an odd thing, as we all know – imaginative, credulous, and sure of its facts before the event; difficult to please and overcritical when the time comes. Reality never seems enough to it, because it has no real idea what it wants . . .
>
> (Alessandro Manzoni, *The Betrothed*)

The history of happiness is no ordinary history, and the subject is by no means ordinary either. The idea of happiness points us to an all-inclusive assessment of a person's condition. It makes a claim, at least, to take into account all considerations about what's desirable and worthwhile. The history of happiness might thus claim to be relevant to everything concerning human, or even other, beings. On both sides, the concept and the history, there seem to be no boundaries within which to work. On various grounds, some contours and limits are called for.

The contours should come from the problem that the concept raises. It attempts and purports to include, as I've just said, everything that's desirable and worthwhile for humans. As the history of happiness shows, however, this totality isn't easy to grasp.

The various aims – and enjoyments, desires, judgments about what's worthwhile, etc. – all of which the notion of happiness is taken to include, seem often to conflict with each other. They seem to conflict with each other in such a way that they can't all be surveyed and evaluated together. Accordingly there might be no non-arbitrary way of constructing a coherent concept out of them. The concept of happiness may simply be the expression of a firm but unrealizable hope for some kind of coherence of aims (see Chapter 7).

A history of happiness as it appears in western philosophy, which is what this book will cover, should contain descriptions of important attempts to fulfill this hope, by somehow harmonizing these elements or systematizing them. Many of these attempts are attached to the word "happiness," and to fairly near equivalents in English and other languages, such as "well-being" and the Greek *eudaimonia*.

Trying to include all of the topics that have been thought relevant to happiness, or all of the people who have said significant things about it, would make impossible the task of a history of happiness, especially a brief one. A great deal has to be left out. I've selected the material to include by its relevance to the philosophical issues surrounding happiness that seem to me most important and interesting. Still, enough is excluded to occupy a much larger book than this one.

The best kind of history of such a philosophical concept is one that concentrates on and confronts interesting and important philosophical problems in which the idea figures. (There's no algorithm for determining which problems are interesting and important; one just has to consider them and see what one thinks and what others think.) There would be no sense in a mere chronological march through the historical periods in which the concept of happiness has been employed. That would only give a hint of the issues connected with the concept that are still worth thinking about. No one ever learns anything about philosophy from the vulgar historicism which says that the understanding of a concept is generated simply by studying its history or its contexts. One has to understand the concept without that, to some extent, before one can begin to know what its history or contexts might tell one about it.

Moreover the connections between the philosophical issues that the concept of happiness raises and the various political, economic, and even cultural events of the periods in which the concept appears aren't even particularly interesting as history. Most of the standard connections are obvious anyway – such as the fact that treatment of the concept in the Middle Ages was associated with Christianity, that this connection was partly loosened in the Renaissance, and so on. Philosophers can, and often do, think of things to discuss that aren't closely tied to their own times; that isn't, really, very difficult for a reasonably intelligent person. So almost every historical context witnesses concepts, and rivalries between concepts and disputes over them, that don't bear any interesting historical relation to other things that went on at the time.

In any case, the connections of this kind that I'll discuss are ones that are integrally connected to deep-seated live problems in the concept as it has been for a very long time under a wide variety of circumstances. By "deep-seated" I don't mean "essential" or "meta-physical" or "timeless" or "eternal." It can just be the case that we have certain concepts and can't put them aside, and that can make certain thoughts obviously wrong. For that to be so, essentiality, and metaphysicalness aren't necessary. Nor is timelessness or eternality. Here we have to do with twenty-five hundred years. That's more than long enough.

Having certain concepts can make certain problems un-get-over-able. (We can forget about this silly false contrast: the idea that if there's no metaphysical basis for settling an issue, then there's nothing to do but have a "conversation" about it.) That becomes clear when one looks at the things that have been said about happiness over the period during which it's been discussed.

Thinking of the history of philosophy as valuable primarily for the sake of thinking about philosophy leads, of course, to a focus on certain philosophical ideas and issues rather than others. That's as it should be. It's as it should be even though it means, when organizing a book, leaving certain interesting things out, among them interesting historical matters. The resources of the history of philosophy are too valuable for philosophy to be allowed to be hostage to encyclopedism, antiquarianism, or historicism.

Most of the important ideas about happiness, and the difficulties that arise from them, were already present in the thinking of the ancient Greeks. Most philosophical questions about happiness that were investigated subsequently – though certainly not all of them – concerned which of those ideas to develop and refine and try to apply, and how to make sense of the obdurately problematic concept itself. That means that the history of happiness, especially when it's brief, has to be to a large extent the ancient history of happiness (though not, for all that, the history only of ancient happiness).

Chapter 1

Introducing the Concept

The word "happy" is familiar. It isn't especially philosophical. It expresses a concept, happiness, that we take ourselves to understand at least to some degree. "Are you happy?," one woman asked another in a coffee house not long ago. "Well . . . ," the second began, "Well, yes, but certain things bother me"; then she was unfortunately interrupted and didn't finish, and when she spoke again it was about something else.

Early in his *Nicomachean Ethics*, Aristotle cites a saying of the Athenian statesman Solon: "Call no one happy until he's dead." Aristotle takes himself to be able to deploy the concept. He elaborates Solon's point. The fortunes of a person's descendants affect his happiness, Aristotle says, at any rate for some time: "[it would] be odd if the fortunes of the descendants did not for *some* time have *some* effect on the happiness of their ancestors" (1100a29–31; emphasis in the original).

Many people nowadays would probably hesitate to say that your grandchildren's fortunes can affect your happiness or your well-being, but most people don't object to saying that what happens to your grandchildren can affect your interests.

The two ideas just mentioned – the women's and Aristotle's – don't fit with each other quite smoothly. But on the other hand they don't belong to two completely different ways of thinking either. It would be clearly wrong, I think, to say that in them the word "happy" expresses two different concepts.

To be sure, the first woman would have been pretty shocked if the other had replied, "Your question's a bit premature, don't you think? Come back and check some time after I've been dead for a while, and see how my grandchildren are doing." On the other hand, the women and Solon wouldn't have any trouble understanding each other's remarks, or the standpoint from which they're made.

Moreover the respective points of the two remarks are plainly connected with each other. It seems obvious that the woman's question about the present, "Are you happy *now*?," has something important to do with what Solon recommended asking about someone after his life is over: "*Was* he happy?" On the other hand it's hard to say just what the connection is.

Moreover the concept clearly seems to be important. Aristotle says that happiness is "the human good," and that everyone aims at it for its own sake and for its own sake alone (*NE* I.7). The role of the concept didn't change much between Aristotle's time and Freud's. Speaking, in *Civilization and its Discontents*, of "what men themselves show . . . to be the purpose and intention of their lives", Freud said,

> What do they demand of life and wish to achieve in it? The answer to this can hardly be in doubt. They strive after happiness; they want to become *happy* and to remain so. (2005: 25)

That's as plausible a thing to say (though some will disagree with it) now as it was then.

But articulating the concept isn't easy. People ask themselves what happiness is, and don't find it easy to answer, even though they think they ought to be able to. When the question's raised, people usually give some examples of things that they want or think are valuable. They also seem to think that they ought to be able to say more – to say something that sums it up. But normally no suitable specification comes to mind. Philosophers and other thinkers, though, have tried to find one.

Plural and Conflicting Aims

When we ask ourselves how we think in normal circumstances about our state or condition, what presents itself to us is a *plurality* of things. They present themselves under various rubrics. One "aims" to do or achieve or acquire certain things. One "wants" this and that and the other. One believes that such-and-such and so-and-so would be "worthwhile" to do or experience. One knows that one would "enjoy" or "welcome" certain things and not others. In each such category a number of things come to mind. All of them are eligible for figuring in one's plans and choices.[1]

The various such things that present themselves to one's attention are always rivals for a person's efforts to gain or enjoy them. They're to some degree in *conflict*, if not intrinsically, then at the very least in competing for the resources and time necessary to gain them or, in the case of projects, to carry them out.

Having a plurality of aims isn't caused by luxury or plenty. Those in need have at least as much reason to have a plurality of aims as those who are well provided. A human being doesn't live by bread alone, or water alone, or sleep alone, or any other single thing. Even keeping alive in extreme straits can require attending to more than one immediate need.

Likewise a certain kind of nostalgic historicist soul might think that it's only in the hectic modern world that people have come to have lots of aims, etc. on their minds. But that's implausible. Even at the simplest level a person attends to various things simultaneously: things like where to place one's feet to avoid rocks in the path and branches at eye level, like whether there's a clearing ahead, like what the sounds around one might signal, what the sky above tells about the coming weather, and so on.

A good account of happiness has to begin with an awareness of the fact of the plurality of aims and conflicts among them. It seems to me that our development of a concept of happiness starts from that awareness. And an articulation of the concept has to incorporate it, and to show how the concept can be won from the plurality, with its potential conflicts, that the awareness sets before us.

Moreover, any philosopher who succeeds in articulating what happiness is has to bring his account of it back into confrontation with the state of the person as he actually is – every person, that is – who finds a plurality of aims presented to him. The philosopher would have to be able to say plausibly, "From your standpoint you can come to see that this, the condition of happiness as I'm describing it, is a good condition to be in" (see Chapter 7).

For whatever condition happiness turns out to be, just about everyone is willing to agree that it's a *good* condition, a condition to go for. So an account of it had better make clear to us as we are that that's so, or at least show how we can come to that point.

But that's not easy to do. With good reason Milton in *Paradise Lost* describes a part of Satan's host who (to adapt slightly)

> . . . reasoned high
> Of Providence, Foreknowledge, Will, and Fate . . . ,
> Of happiness and final misery . . . ,
> And found no end, in wandering mazes lost.
> (II.558–9, 563, 561)

If understanding happiness is difficult for infernal philosophers, it isn't easy for others either. If we wanted or valued just one thing, then saying what happiness is would be much easier than it is.

Note

1   A point of terminology. Some recent philosophy uses a single notion, "desire," for a person's attitude toward all or most of the kinds of conditions that I've mentioned. I prefer to talk multifariously, of what one *aims at, wants, believes worthwhile or good, expects to enjoy or would welcome,* etc. The explanatory value of covering the field of all these things under a single

Introducing the Concept

label seems to me dubious. It's also certainly not in accord with ordinary thinking. In general I use multifarious terms, although for brevity, I often use the word "aim" (or "aims, etc."), and sometimes "consideration," as stand-ins for all of them. The points that I'll make usually cover them all.

Chapter 2

Conflicts, Perspectives, and the Identification of Happiness

Where We Start

As so often, Plato made the first move. In his *Gorgias* and *Republic* he took his start from the recognition that we have plural and conflicting desires, aims, impulses, etc., and that somehow we have to deal with that fact. He can hardly have been the first to notice the fact of plurality and conflict, but he was the first to react to it systematically.

In the fifth century BC, Gorgias the Greek Sophist, whose name Plato used as the title of his dialogue, appears to have adopted the position that a person's well-being consists in, to put it broadly, "getting what(ever) one wants." Or anyway that's the view that Plato attributes to Gorgias in that dialogue.

Gorgias advertised himself as a teacher of rhetoric. He could, he claimed, teach people to "be persuasive about all subjects," though he said that those subjects needn't be anything about which either he or his pupils knew anything at all (458e, 459c). With this capacity a person would have, in words that Plato put into Gorgias' mouth,

> the ability to persuade with his speeches both judges in law courts, councilors in council meetings, and assemblymen in assembly meetings,

or in any other political gathering . . . [and so would] have the doctor as your slave and the physical trainer too. As for your financial expert, he'll end up making more money for someone other than himself, namely for you, in fact, if you've got the ability to speak and to persuade the mob. (*Gorgias* 452d–e)

What you get from all this, in Gorgias' view, is the ability to get whatever you want. This, Plato makes him say, is "the greatest good."

Gorgias doesn't tell you what to want, or what he believes you *should* want. That, he maintains, is your business. He doesn't believe that he needs to tell you what to want, in order to tell you what your well-being consists in or to help you get it. Whatever things you happen to want, your well-being consists in getting them.

Later in the *Gorgias* Plato introduces the character "Callicles" (not, it seems, a real person, or at any rate certainly not under his real name) to articulate Gorgias' position further, thus:

How could a man prove to be happy if he's enslaved to anyone at all? Rather, this is what's admirable and just by nature . . . that the man who'll live rightly ought to allow his appetites to get as large as possible and not restrain them. And when they get as large as possible, he ought to be capable of devoting himself to them through his bravery and intelligence, and to fill them with whatever he may have an appetite for at the time. (491e–492a)

Living "rightly" means here: getting the greatest possible satisfaction of the greatest desires, as they arise. The greatest satisfactions come from satisfying the most intense desires. When a desire appears or grows strong, then it should be satisfied.

Plato doesn't deny that people are in fact normally confronted with a plurality of desires. In the *Republic* he expounds a theory of the human personality – or "soul," as he puts it – according to which it's made up of many "parts" (of which the main ones are three in number: reason, spirit, and a whole collection of "appetites").

In a general way and apart from the particular details of his theory of the soul, Plato's right about this. What presents itself to us is usually, as we live our lives, a more or less sprawling plurality: aims, enjoyments, judgments and thoughts about what's worthwhile, desires, and so on. These things don't present themselves to a person's everyday consciousness as a single well-defined totality or whole.

Before taking up Plato's reaction to (what he presents as) Gorgias' view, I must mention that the view that well-being consists in getting what you want reappears in various forms throughout the history of happiness.

In Greek antiquity a version of it was proposed by a contemporary of Plato, Aristippus of Cyrene, whose works are almost wholly lost and who's hardly known any more, and another version was suggested by Hobbes, who paid attention to the problems in the position that Plato had pointed out (see Chapter 3). With further modifications and elaborations, a much more systematic adaptation of the idea crops up in so-called "desire-satisfaction" theories of well-being, sometimes linked to "the theory of preference" as it's been developed by philosophers and economists (Chapters 3 and 6).

Hobbes's formulation of the idea in the mid-seventeenth century is nowadays the best known. Hobbes used the word "felicity," which (like "well-being" and several other words) is pretty nearly equivalent, in most people's usage, to "happiness." Hobbes characterized felicity in these words:

> Continual success in obtaining those things which a man from time to time desireth, that is to say, continual prospering, is that men call FELICITY. (*Leviathan*, ch. 6)

On this picture (which doesn't give the whole of Hobbes's view), a person has a "continual" stream of desires, and happiness consists in satisfying them as they pop up (see Chapters 3, 4, 7).

In the *Gorgias* Plato launches a criticism of the position espoused there by Gorgias and Callicles. To begin with, he makes Callicles feel uncomfortable about the fact that his aims can often conflict. In particular there are conflicts between certain desires of his and views that he has about which desires it's good to have. Callicles turns out to be unwilling to advocate the greatest possible satisfaction of just *any* desires. He regards some desires as shameful or trivial or both.

Plato has the character Socrates challenge Callicles (and by implication Gorgias) as follows:

> Tell me now whether a man who has an itch and scratches it and can scratch to his heart's content, scratch his whole life long, can also live happily. (494d)

Callicles recoils at this suggestion. He's simply unwilling to regard the condition of someone who continually scratches an itch as a good condition, even if it really were the most intense satisfaction of the most urgent desire that he has at the time or through his life.

Virtually everyone, Plato thinks, has such scruples about which of their wants are fulfilled. They *don't want* certain desires to be satisfied – certainly not to the exclusion of others. In fact they desire certain of their desires *not* to be satisfied, or think that they *shouldn't* be. And they willingly accept recommendations to curb them:

> doctors generally allow a person to fill up his appetites, to eat when he's hungry, for example, or drink when he's thirsty as much as he wants to when he's in good health, but when he's sick they practically never allow him to fill himself with what he has an appetite for . . . (505a)

The man with the itch whom Plato cites against Callicles is like this. He certainly wants to scratch, but he doesn't want to be a person who spends his whole life scratching an itch. Callicles' view involves him in an inconsistency: he aims to satisfy all his desires immediately, and to allow all his desires to grow unrestrained so that they can be satisfied; and on occasion he desires to scratch; but he also (Plato makes him realize) desires not to spend all his time satisfying that particular desire. In one fell swoop Plato makes him see both (a) that there are certain desires that he wants not to have (too much of), because he regards them as contemptible, and (b) that his position involves a kind of inconsistency.

By the way, Plato here – and even more explicitly in the *Republic* – makes a point that Joseph Butler stressed in the seventeenth century (Chapter 4). People in fact have desires that are, so to speak, *about* other desires. That is, a normal person has desires whose subject matter concerns how he wants his desires to be, or how he wants them to be satisfied, if at all. ("Second-order desires" is the phrase that's sometimes used by philosophers nowadays, and a contemporary example is of the person who desires to smoke but also desires not to desire to smoke, or at least desires that his desire to smoke not be effective.) Thus, aside from being concerned simply with states of affairs external to themselves or their bodies, people are also spectators and judges of themselves, and accordingly have self-referential, self-reflective aims.

Where to Go from Where We Start

Plato thought that the state of having conflicting aims, so far from being "the greatest good" as Gorgias claimed, is a bad state to be in. We can start to see his reasons if we consider everyday deliberation about what to do.

In ordinary deliberation, a short-term conflict of aims is the occasion for thought. A person can't do everything at once. When two immediate aims conflict, you have to decide what to do now. Even when two projects aren't intrinsically opposed, starting on both of them simultaneously usually won't be possible. Life is full of postponements, and the preferring of one aim over another for the moment. A similar situation obtains in the smoker's case, who wants something but wishes he didn't. Is now the moment to smoke, or the moment to start giving up?

This kind of case tells us that a conflict of aims, or a plurality of aims that we can't embark on fulfilling simultaneously, has to be *dealt with*, somehow. Such cases don't, though, tell us *how* to deal with conflict. They don't tell us whether one aim should be abandoned, or whether the conflicting aims should be coordinated (one being postponed until the other's taken care of), or whether their respective merits should somehow be measured against each other, or in some further way. Indeed, these cases don't even tell us that conflicts of aims are a bad thing. They only show us that a conflict usually has to be the occasion for *some* kind of thought about what to do.

For the most part we deal with conflicts locally and in the short term. You have several things that you should do, and this afternoon is the perfect time for each of them, but not long enough for all of them. So you pick and choose, selecting one to start with, others to do later, and others, perhaps, to be put off until next week. Planning often has this shape.

Failing to plan, it would appear, can often make a mess of things. Plato was especially averse to that kind of outcome. Here's his portrait of the "democratic man":

> [living] out his life . . . day by day, indulging the appetite of the day, now drinking wine and giving himself over to the sensuous pleasure of the flute, and then again drinking only water and dieting, and at one time exercising his body; and sometimes idling and neglecting all his affairs and at another time appearing to occupy himself with philosophy; and often he goes in for politics and jumps up and says and does whatever comes into his head. (*Republic* 561c–d)

Not being able to deal thoughtfully with conflict and multiplicity of aims, Plato thinks, makes in every situation for poor results.

Planning can extend beyond the merely local and beyond the short term. We can plan for a month or a year or a stretch of years or for a whole life, insofar as we can foresee its rough extent. Some people even plan for longer stretches, extending beyond their lifetimes. As most people view the matter, and as Solon and Aristotle recommended seeing it, an overview of one's whole life or somewhat more is what thinking about one's overall happiness consists in.

Taking this sort of overview involves plurality and potential conflicts with a vengeance. Exactly what the overview should lead one to conclude is still open, from what we've seen so far. In fact, the number of proposals made by philosophers, as to what overall happiness is, is extremely large.

On this matter, Aristotle had an especially stringent-seeming suggestion. He says, in his other treatise on ethics, the so-called *Eudemian Ethics*,

> we must urge everyone who has the power to live according to his own choice to set up for himself an object . . . to aim at – honor or reputation or wealth or culture – with reference to which he will perform all his actions. For not to have one's life organized by reference to some end is foolish. (1214b6–11)

That's one way to deal with the plurality of aims over the long term: pick out a single aim as in some sense pre-eminent. But this isn't the only way to deal with the issue.

We can think of an all-embracing overview of a person's aims, etc., as dealing with or taking into consideration *all* of one's aims, desires, values, and so on. Once again, "taking them all into consideration" here doesn't mean fulfilling them. It might include, for instance, rejecting some or even most of them, or limiting them, or the like. The point is merely that if you consider your whole life or some similarly wide domain over which you might plan, and consider also the aims etc. that you actually have, then you'll certainly have to do some planning and adjusting. Your actual life quite certainly doesn't contain room for all of your aims, and some of them are inconsistent with others quite apart from that limitation.

Many philosophers have thought that if you take all aims into consideration in an overview of a person's condition, one of the results will be an *overall assessment* or *evaluation* of it. "Am I happy?," I can ask, or "Was he happy?" or, "How happy am I?"; or one can say things like, "She was much happier than her sister." The evaluation may be rough, but it can be made – that's the assumption underlying Plato's view, and it's widely shared. The word "happy," then, can be thought of as expressing a positive assessment (or in some cases an optimal one).

We acquire or develop the concept of happiness, it seems plausible to assert, by starting with the idea of taking a relatively narrow set of local aims into consideration in the way indicated, and then extending that idea to include a whole life or some similar extent, along with all of the aims that one might have in it. And then we try to figure out how all of those aims might be taken into consideration – whether coordinated, for instance, or cut down or selected – within that extent.

The concept of happiness, then, can be thought of as what results when we figure that out – if we can. Acquiring the concept means acquiring, first, the idea of trying to figure out how to take all of those aims into consideration, and, at the ideal limit, succeeding at doing so. It's the outcome, that means, of trying to apply to all of our aims the same kind of planning that we engage in when we deal in the short term – e.g., an afternoon – with a plurality of conflicting considerations.

The concept of happiness is accordingly the analogue of the concept of a successful way of dealing with a shorter period and fewer aims. Deliberating about how to be happy is therefore also the analogue of deliberating about how to deal with a smaller group of aims over a shorter time span. That seems to be the obvious upshot of Plato's way responding to Callicles in the *Gorgias*.

Given that much, it's pretty clear what an *account* of the concept of happiness would aspire to do. It would aspire to state, insofar as that's possible, how the whole multiplicity of our aims, etc., should best be taken into consideration in an overview of a life or other relevant period or domain.

This is what all historical accounts of happiness try to do, one way or another and to one extent or another. The fact that we have the idea of *trying* to do this shows that, at least to some extent, we have the concept of happiness.

On the other hand some philosophers think that we *can't* figure out how all of those aims can be taken into account, because it's obvious that they can't be. Sometimes Hobbes's words suggest such a thought:

> [T]here is no such *Finis ultimus* [utmost aim] nor *Summum bonum* [greatest good] as is spoken of in the books of the old moral philosophers. (*Leviathan*, ch. 11)

Likewise Kant, in the *Critique of Practical Reason*:

> [I]t is impossible for the most insightful and at the same time most powerful, but nonetheless finite, being to frame here a determinate concept of what it is that he really wills. (Bk II, ch. ii)

At the very least, Hobbes and Kant have severe doubts about whether we can form a *clear* conception of happiness, and about that they may well be right (see Chapter 7).

A perspicuous account of happiness could be expected to explain, in a general way, how all aims can be taken into consideration in assessing or evaluating a person's condition. The account would include a way of saying, on the basis of all those considerations, what makes that condition better or worse. The account might explain what it is for a condition to be *optimal*. These are things that Plato and other philosophers try to do (see below and Chapters 4 and 7). It might involve explaining what the role of each aim is in the best condition that a human being might be in (perhaps taking account of details of the circumstances). It would also make clear why aims whose fulfillment has no place in such a condition – according to some, certain grotesque pleasures – are excluded from it, and why other aims – like watching professional wrestling on television – have only a very limited place.

Couldn't a philosophical account of happiness be expected to go even further, and to give concrete directions about how a person might become happy, or happier? Some of the history of happiness shows attempts to do that – not just a general specification of how varying considerations should be taken into account, but direct instructions about what to do. A good many Greek philosophers (Epicurus, Stoics such as Epictetus) make this effort. Plenty of philosophers themselves say that it's the role of philosophers, which they're shirking when they don't offer concrete advice, or at least methods of self-help.

But – sad to say – philosophers as a group are bad at this (even worse than they are at thinking about politics). Plato provided one of the earliest illustrations of the fact in his *Republic*, and his failed attempts (as it seems) to put its ideas into practice. Philosophers' concrete advice about how to become happy isn't any better (in fact, it's probably worse) than that of the average person. They generally don't know enough of the relevant facts, and they don't have the right temperament. In this state of affairs, there's no point incorporating this role into anyone's idea of the function of philosophers.

On the other hand, almost every person – philosopher or not – feels constrained to form *some* conception, however, vague, of happiness as it applies to himself. That is, he feels constrained to figure out some way in which the plurality of aims should be taken into consideration, whatever the exact result of that consideration is. An individual even feels constrained to allow this conception, in all its indefiniteness, to play *some* kind of role in his deliberations, even if it's only in the vague background.

Extensions of Happiness: a Brief Digression

Until now I've talked about the happiness or well-being of individual human beings. Other things are often called "happy" too, for example: groups of people, societies, communities, nations, and so on, as well as cats and dogs, and (by Lucretius) crops in the field. Of these things, the first three have in the history of thought made the most emphatic claim to be called "happy" or "unhappy" in the same sense as individuals. Plato's *Republic* tries – unsuccessfully – to explain the well-being and also the justice of a city-state (*polis*) in exactly the same breath, and way, as the well-being of the person.

The happiness of a community or society is different enough from the happiness of an individual to fall outside of the purview of this book. That seems obvious. Even if communities and societies have goals and make decisions and undertake actions, as they do, and are entities "over and above" their members or citizens, that doesn't show that *all* such notions apply to them in the same way or sense as they apply to their constituent persons. For one thing, what goes to constitute the happiness of a society in relation to the condition of its parts is very different from what goes to constitute the happiness of an individual. It's true that we have some of the same difficulties in understanding the happiness of a group as we have in understanding that of a person. But that fact itself can be better seen by focusing first on the latter notion.

A Single Evaluation

What we can ask from a philosophical account of happiness, I've said, is that it explain clearly how all aims, desires, etc., can be pulled together and taken into consideration in assessing or evaluating a person's condition.

Does the same account hold good for everyone? Does the same account hold good for a given individual through the varying circumstances of his or her life? Or is the happiness of one person through and through different from the happiness of another, and can the happiness of one person at one time be fundamentally different from his or her happiness at another?

When people try to "pull together" a plurality of considerations, to ask "how things are going" or "how someone's life has gone," there's a striking fact about what they do, which is reflected in the whole notion of happiness and its history. People have an almost irresistible tendency to try to answer this in a single way. This is true even though everyone knows that in some way their happiness has various different aspects. Nevertheless, almost everyone tries to find a single answer, which will embrace all of the considerations that have anything to do with the assessment of their condition, and will sum up completely how well they're doing or how well they've done. There are, to be sure, some exceptions to this generalization, including some important philosophers (Chapters 2 and 4). To most ways of thinking, however, the word "happiness" is used to cover a single all-embracing evaluation of an individual's state.

Not everyone agrees, of course, that all individuals do or should employ the same standard of assessment. A certain sort of relativism about happiness holds, for instance, that no unique measure of happiness is suitable for everyone. They'll readily say, "You evaluate your life your way, and I'll evaluate mine my way."

This kind of relativism seems fairly natural. It seems to quite a few people a good deal more natural than an analogous relativism about right and wrong. It doesn't seem outlandish to suggest that if I'd been born a Norwegian or a Tibetan or an Angolan, or had been much more intelligent or fit than I am, a very different standard would apply to my condition. This relativist idea can seem correct even if one holds that standards of fairness or justice are in some substantial way the same for all.

Nevertheless, when people confine their attention to themselves as they actually are, they normally *aren't* ready to say, "I should assess my life this way on Tuesday, and that way on Wednesday, and both ways are equally adequate, and it doesn't make sense to ask about which assessment is right."

On the contrary, people want to be able to say direct things about themselves, such as, "I'm doing well," or "I need to do better," or, "If so-and-so happens, then my life will be ruined" or ". . . will be a triumph," or "If this keeps up I'll have made a mess of things." A person looks for a single evaluation of his condition to focus on, even if he doesn't exactly know how it ought to be constructed. That's why he thinks that there should be a single answer to *his* question, "What does my happiness consist in?," even if he thinks that another person might reasonably answer the question according to different standards.

Evidence on this point is easy to find in the history of happiness. Aristotle provides an especially good illustration of the propensity to look for a single way to assess one's own condition overall. Going somewhat against his usual tendency to say that words (including "good") can be used in different ways, he *wasn't* prepared to say that about the word "happiness" (*eudaimonia*) as applied to human beings. He didn't allow a plurality of evaluations to be given for various kinds of human happiness. He wanted to identify human happiness, to say what it is, not to characterize a variety of things that it can be.

When he comes to say what he thinks happiness is, he never admits the option of holding that it can simultaneously be considered to be various things. He said that human happiness is

> activity of the soul in accordance with excellence, *or if there's more than one* excellence, in accordance with *the best and most complete* excellence. (*Nicomachean Ethics* 1098a17–18, my emphasis)

That is, he *didn't* say, "or if there is more than one excellence, *then 'happiness' signifies many different things.*"

Aristotle assumes, that is, that even if there might be pressure to say that there exist a plurality of things called "happiness" (see further Chapter 4), he should resist it and count happiness as one single thing.

Consider another even more striking example. Why does Christianity have the idea of a Judgment *Day*, rather than, say, a whole Judgment Week or a Judgment Month, made up of lots of judgment days for different judgments about different categories of evaluation, like different events in the Olympic Games? Why, in other words, does it seem appropriate for a religion of this sort to have a single, all-in judgment? The question – which hardly if ever arises in people's minds – points up how thoroughly ingrained the propensity is to think that the evaluation of a person's condition can be made in one fell swoop.

Platonic Harmony

To many philosophers, the obvious way to react to the plurality of considerations and their potential conflicts, as so far described, is to think that happiness must be a *harmony* of aims, etc. This was certainly Plato's view. Indeed, he seems to have thought it unavoidable. In his description of "the completely good man" (*Rep.* 427e), he describes the harmony of such a person's soul or personality. Such a person

> doesn't allow any part of himself to do the work of another part, or let the various elements in him interfere with each other. He organizes what's really his own well, and rules himself. He puts himself in order, is his own friend, and harmonizes the . . . parts of himself like . . . limiting notes in a musical chord. He binds those parts together, and any others in between, and from having been many he becomes entirely one, moderate and harmonious. (*Rep.* 443d)

Plato's thinking is guided by two considerations, both of which turned out to be highly influential. One was the thought that a conflict among aims is bad for a person. The other was that unless happiness is some kind of harmony, no clear account of it can be articulated or understood.

On the first point, Plato's reasons were these: In the first place, he thought, a person whose aims aren't consistent is doomed to frustration. That's of course because if two aims can't be satisfied together, then one of them will be frustrated. And frustration is normally bad. Thus Plato describes the "prison house" in which the "tyrannical" personality "is pent, being . . . filled with multitudinous and manifold terrors and appetites . . . greedy and avid of spirit as he is" (*Rep.* 579b). The tyrant's unhappiness is brought about largely by his having desires that stand in each other's way.

Second, Plato believed that conflict within a person's soul betokens a failure of some of its parts to perform their "natural function." Plato believed that each element of a human personality has a function that it naturally performs. Hunger, for instance, has the natural function of causing an intake of food that will keep the body in good condition. However, the "bodily" desires tend to encroach on each other. For example, a glutton's desire to eat might move him to forgo exercise, and so no longer be in good shape. Plato seems to hold that the performance of natural function is a good thing.

Third, Plato holds that if a person is subject to conflict, then that's generally because his reason hasn't successfully governed his personality. In particular his reason hasn't governed and organized his desires. In that case, not only is his reason not performing its natural function – which is to organize and direct the personality – but in addition, *that* means (Plato believes) that the person's reason doesn't have a clear, consistent conception of the harmony of all desires to which a person should conform. That's a failure of reason, a kind of irrationality.

This last point makes it clear why Plato thought that unless happiness is a harmony of aims, no intelligible account of it can be given – by a philosopher or anybody else.

Like many philosophers, Plato assumes that the whole point of articulating the concept of happiness is to give people guidance. I've already pointed out that we can think of the concept as arising from our efforts to deliberate about what to do. The concept of happiness is the analogue, writ large, of what we do when we plan for the short run. So, it seems to follow, an account of happiness ought to be usable as a guide. It ought, that is, to guide us through the uncertainties that we encounter when we think about our various sometimes conflicting aims and desires. It ought to tell us what to do when they give contrary instructions.

If the concept of happiness is to be such a guide, it seems also to follow that it must specify a consistent set of aims. If you're told to do *A* and *B* but they can't both be done, then you haven't been told what to do. You've got to decide on your own whether to do *A* or *B* or for that matter something else. So it appears that a conflicting specification of aims can't articulate what happiness is, if it's to do its job of guiding. That makes it useless for the philosopher or anyone else to offer it. That's how Plato reasons.

That's exactly the reason why Plato rejected Gorgias' account of happiness as "getting what(ever) you want." If that's what Gorgias tells you to do, and if your wants are inconsistent as most people's are, then Gorgias hasn't after all made a recommendation that's coherent and that you could follow. That's the position that Callicles is in. If he itches for his whole life and wants to scratch, Gorgias' view tells him to scratch, and that that's "the greatest good." But Callicles doesn't think that being in that state is a good thing.

Change and Harmony

When I've talked about conflicts and harmony of aims, I've mostly illustrated the idea with cases of inconsistency and consistency between desires, etc., that are present to consciousness simultaneously: *synchronic conflicts*. But there are also conflicts over time – *diachronic conflicts* – to deal with. These play a significant role in Plato's thinking. They'll also be important later in connection with dynamic conceptions of happiness (Chapter 7).

Plato doesn't see the need for harmony only in response to synchronic conflicts. In the *Gorgias* and the *Republic* he's also occupied with diachronic ones. A human being, after all, is extended in time. Moreover people have aims, and also perspectives on their aims and their fulfillment, that aren't always temporally constant. We don't just live in the present, aware now of the things that we want now. Our relation to the world alters, and our view of what we want from it looks temporally backwards and forwards in a complex way.

Late in the evening you want to get up at 6:00 the next morning. When that time arrives, however, you're sleepy. Moreover you wish you hadn't set the alarm the previous evening. And you want to sleep till 9:00. In fact, getting up at 6:00 seems like a terrible idea, and the considerations that urged you to do it seem nugatory. But then when you finally wake up at 10:00, you're no longer sleepy, but you side with what you did the evening before and you wish you'd gotten up at 6:00, or at the latest 8:00, and you think it was a good idea.

The picture is made more elaborate by pleasures and displeasures of anticipation (many of the latter being fears), and also pleasures and displeasures of retrospection. In the evening you're pleased at the thought of your getting up at such a diligently early hour and seeing the sun rise; and at 10:00 a.m., looking back, you're ashamed that you misjudged your capacities so badly, but you also look back with pleasure at the feeling of the covers on top of you.

The general worry raised by points of this kind revolves around questions about *perspective*. Which viewpoint to take as governing when assessing one's condition or deciding what to do? "Who should be referee or boss," some people want to ask, "myself at 6:00 or 8:00 or 9:00 or 10:00, or at some other time?" If "my" happiness is to be measured by the achievement of "my" aims, does that mean the aims of 6:00 or of one of the other times?

Plato recommends a general type of answer to this kind of question: that the judgment be made from a neutral, all-encompassing perspective. By taking up this perspective, he holds, we can avoid the partiality of the present moment, or of any particular moment, "stumbling like children, clapping one's hands to the stricken spot and wasting time in wailing." Instead,

> it is best to keep quiet as far as possible in calamity and not to chafe and repine, because we cannot know what is really good and evil in such things . . . and nothing in mortal life is worthy of very great concern. (*Rep.* 604c)

Plato thinks that the evaluations that are generated by this latter outlook have a special status. Since they're not forced by perceptions at particular time, they're in a sense objective. These are the judgments that should govern our evaluations and actions, and enable an appropriate harmonization of aims.

In this way Plato ends up espousing an integration of the personality and its aims that's both synchronic and diachronic. To achieve this result the *Republic* favors a person's having a single *function* or *occupation*. In the *Gorgias* he speaks for an orderly arrangement of desires and satisfactions. He urges us to consider

> painters . . . or house-builders or shipwrights or any other craftsmen you please, and see how each one puts what he does into a certain structure, and forces one thing to be suited to another and to fit with it, until the entire object is put together in an organized and structured way. (503e–504a)

The *Republic* is built around this same idea, that an individual who's in a good condition (like a city-state as well) has "harmonized" the parts of his personality, "and [has] linked and bound all three together and made of himself a unit, one man instead of many, self-controlled and in unison" (443d–e).

This is the kind of person whom Plato regards as happy, in contrast to the fragmented personality of the democratic man.

The idea of a neutral perspective that Plato first developed has its heirs in the long-lived, traditional concept of prudence. As prudence is standardly conceived it doesn't demand that all of a person's activities be organized around a single function or activity, in the fashion that Plato pressed for. One of the things that it does require, though, is that all of the times in a person's life be in some sense treated as being on a par.

Usually the emphasis here falls on times well in the future, but only because normal people tend to neglect them in their plans. The commonsensical idea is encouraged – as it is in children by their parents – that the present shouldn't command a person's attention more than even one's remote future does. Thus Spinoza urges that the time at which one encounters something good or bad should be indifferent to a person, because one regards everything from a neutral standpoint:

> In so far as the mind conceives things in accordance with the dictate of reason, it is equally affected whether the idea be of a thing that is future, past, or present

for:

> Whatever the mind conceives when it is led by reason it conceives under the same species of eternity, i.e. of necessity ... and it is affected with the same certainty. ... Therefore, whether the idea be of a thing that is future, past, or present, the mind conceives of the thing with the same necessity, and is affected with the same certainty. (*Ethics*, IV. Prop. 62)

Sidgwick presents another version of the idea. He enunciates a principle of prudence, and tries to give it a basis of roughly the same kind as what Plato urged against Callicles:

> [The notion of] one's 'good on the whole' ... suggests a principle ... of impartial concern for all parts of our conscious life ... [or] 'that Hereafter *as such* is to be regarded neither less nor more than Now'. (*The Methods of Ethics*, p. 381)

A Fondness for Conflict

Plato greatly overestimated how obviously right his account of happiness would appear. For one thing, his particular conception of the harmony of the personality (and of the city-state) turned out to be much less convincing than he expected. Even more important, the same was true of the idea of harmony itself. A substantial number of philosophers have over the years rejected the thesis that the more harmony, the better.

Aristotle was the first. Within the sphere of politics he denied that the best city-state was the most unified. Speaking of the character Socrates in the *Republic*, he says:

> I'm speaking of the premise from which Socrates' argument proceeds: "the greater the unity of the city-state [*polis*], the better'. Isn't it plain that a city-state may at length have so much unity that it's no longer a city-state? For the nature of a city-state is to be a plurality. ... So we shouldn't attain the greatest unity even if we could, for it would be the destruction of the city-state. (*Politics* 1261a15–23)

Aristotle holds much the same view about the individual. He says that a bad man will be subject to conflicts in a way that the good man won't, but he doesn't exempt the good man from all conflicts. In particular, a human being has a "double nature" (as it was later put): a practical side and a theoretical one. The activities of the two can't be fully reconciled, and so a choice has to be made between one or the other, so that some of the value of the one or the other is lost (*NE* X.6–8; see Chapter 4).

Whereas Aristotle attaches some value to freedom from conflict and to focus on a single aim, subsequent philosophers have diverged from Plato's view even further. Some thinkers simply don't regard this sort of integration as important to a person's state. Others hold that conflict of aims, and certainly a multiplicity of them, is in some ways desirable; some even go so far as to say that life is very much less good without conflict. When it's objected from Plato's side that opposed aims lead to frustration of at least some of them, these thinkers respond either by saying that frustration of aims is itself to be welcomed, at least to some extent, or that having opposed aims doesn't, after all, always augment it.

In the *Gorgias*, Plato makes it look as though, when Gorgias and Callicles say that the best human condition is getting what one wants, it simply hasn't *occurred* to them that an unplanned effort to fulfill one's aims might lead to difficulties. Furthermore Plato seems to take to be pretty obvious that it's logically incoherent for a person not to try to minimize conflicts. At any rate, Callicles isn't made to show any concern for whether or not his aims fit together. We can perhaps consider him the prototype of the thinker who doesn't think that the fitting together of one's aims is worth caring about, or who does think, affirmatively, that it's better *not* to care about it.

In criticizing Callicles, in fact, it looks as though Plato let himself off too easily. Callicles happens to have inconsistent wants, because he's ashamed of a life that involves nothing but the satisfaction of scratching an itch and so doesn't want to have that want, or at least not very much of it. But suppose he doesn't mind having, and satisfying, that desire throughout his life. That seems possible. And if someone were free of desires that supervise other desires the best condition might seem, for such a person, to consist in getting what he wanted after all.

Plato appears to believe, though, that there just couldn't be a human being who's free of supervisory desires, not just that Callicles doesn't happen to be one. Plato maintains that all human beings have a reasoning part, however puny it might be. And that part of the personality makes judgments about the values of the desires of the other parts.

In opposition to Plato, Aristippus maintained that a person could indeed be free of supervisory desires, and that such people were happier than those who supervise, control, or filter their own aims.

One of the few surviving quotations from the works of Aristippus is this one:

> [Aristippus] believed that our end is different from "happiness." Our end is particular pleasures, whereas happiness is a structure of particular pleasures, which includes past and future ones. A particular pleasure is choiceworthy for itself, whereas happiness isn't

choiceworthy for itself but for the particular pleasures. That pleasure is our end is shown to be plausible by the facts that from childhood we're drawn to it without having chosen it in advance, and that once we obtain it we don't seek anything further, and we don't avoid anything in this way except its contrary, pain. (Diogenes Laertius, *Lives of the Philosophers*, II.88)

Aristippus is significant as a representative of an extreme position. He denies the need for any structuring of desires or aims at all, whether a "filter" or anything else. In effect he denies, at the least, that consistency of desires from one time to another is anything to be concerned about. The best state, he holds, is an entirely unstructured series of satisfactions, of what have sometimes been called "now for now" desires: desires that one has at a particular moment for some state of affairs to hold right away. These are the desires and satisfactions that we have as children. We should be like children, in that we simply shouldn't make programmatic judgments about what our first-order desires should be. We should simply take our first-order desires as they come (and go), and try to satisfy them as best we can.

Aristippus objects to using the word "happiness" for the condition that he recommends. For he believes that that word has the connotation, established by prior philosophical theories like Plato's, of an organized structure of satisfactions, rather than simply a series of them determined by the happenstance of what desires arise and which of them are satisfied. Instead Aristippus uses the word "end." The satisfaction of these desires is what we aim at, without any organizing structure to govern them. (Perhaps we should say that he recommends having one supervisory aim, namely, the aim of not having any "censorship" of one's ground-level desires; but the logical tangles potentially occasioned by this idea are best ignored here.)

Callicles has a number of more recent intellectual heirs too. Nietzsche is one of them. A sometime classical scholar, Nietzsche plainly wanted his readers to notice the similarity between him and Callicles. He therefore mounts a defense of the clash of desires that's often rather Calliclean in tone.

The important idea that one sees in Nietzsche's writings is that clashes of desires can be desirable. They are so when they're a source of a certain sort of exhilaration, and also a spur to the kind of accomplishment that Nietzsche thinks is grand and impressive. Conflicts of aims prevent life from settling into a humdrum routine, and combat the kind of "happiness" that most people want. Nietzsche speaks of the difference between "weak human beings" and others):

> Happiness appears to [weak human beings], in agreement with a tranquillizing medicine and way of thought (for instance, Epicurean or Christian), pre-eminently as the happiness of resting, of being undisturbed, or satiety, of finally attained unity, as a "sabbath of sabbaths," to speak with the holy rhetorician Augustine, who was himself such a human being.
>
> But when the opposition and war in such a nature have the effect of one more charm and incentive of life – and if, moreover, in addition to his powerful and irreconcilable drives, a real mastery and subtlety in waging war against oneself, in other words, self-control, self-outwitting, has been inherited or cultivated too, then those magical, incomprehensible and unfathomable ones arise – those enigmatic men predestined for victory and seduction. (*Beyond Good and Evil*, §200)

Nietzsche also has no interest in the theoretical project of giving a complete specification of the kind of condition that he welcomes being in. He believes that engaging in that project itself leads away from doing what's worth a thinker's time. He also isn't fond of the word "happiness" as a label for the condition that he's concerned to be in, since for him that word means merely "the happiness of resting, of not being disturbed, or satiety, of finally attained unity." You can count him as rejecting harmony and happiness, too, in the sense in which Plato favored them (though of course you might say that he strives for happiness in a broader, less restricted sense).

Nietzsche has some pretty definite reasons for being hostile to Platonic-style harmony. Knowing that one's striving for things that are hard or even impossible to reconcile generates tension in a person, and a sense of the difficulty of one's undertaking. Nietzsche *likes* that, and is for it. He takes it as a sign that one's extending oneself and responding to a challenge. That causes exhilaration. Even frustration can have results that a strong person should welcome.

Furthermore, trying to put aside any concern with whether one's aims are consistent means putting aside conceptual fussiness. Nietzsche likes that too. Furthermore he seems also to have doubts – though he doesn't articulate them fully (one wouldn't expect him to) – about whether one *can* specify just what consistency of aims amounts to. If he did, then that's something that he shared with Kant, as will emerge (Chapter 4).

Joining forces with Nietzsche in this (as we can roughly call it) Calliclean tradition – of welcoming conflict of aims at least to some degree, or at least not being wholeheartedly in favor of harmony of aims as Plato was – are many writers associated with the Romantic movement. Byron's a good example:

> But long ere scarce a third of his [life] passed by,
> Worse than adversity the Childe befell:
> He felt the fullness of satiety . . .
> (*Childe Harold's Pilgrimage*, I.iv)

Since conflicts of aims can bring frustration, someone who favors conflict might favor frustration too. Sure enough, writers such as Byron, indifferent to threats of paradox, try to suggest how that might be.

Ralph Waldo Emerson intended something similar to Callicles' attitude – and certainly in opposition to Plato's objections to conflicts among a person's aims – with his famous remark:

A foolish consistency is the hobgoblin of little minds, adored by little statesmen and philosophers and divines. With consistency a great soul has simply nothing to do. ("Self-reliance")

Obviously the potential for inconsistency shows itself in all such ideas, but it's characteristic of these thinkers to thumb their noses at it. Those of a different cast of mind can of course always try to smooth away the paradoxes. One way is to agree with Nietzsche, for example, that it can be exciting and more conducive to happiness overall to have some aims that clash, and even to feel the unease that comes from that, but to go on to say that when the desire for this excitement is taken into account, the overall scheme of desires is actually consistent, and indeed is a straightforward maximization of satisfaction (see Chapter 3). And one can even say that it spoils this satisfaction to have, let alone to cultivate, an awareness that it really involves no contradiction. But we don't need to follow this line of thought further here.

Not all philosophers strongly influenced by Plato have been as worried as he was about conflicts of aims, or so insistent on a strict harmony of the personality, although they haven't gone as far as Nietzsche or Emerson. One of these more moderate Platonist philosophers is Pico della Mirandola.

As his description of the democratic man (quoted above) showed, Plato was repelled by the plurality of aims and even of personalities that he saw in the democratic type of man. But some quite Platonic thinkers have been attracted by that very plurality, or what one can think of as versatility, which runs against Plato's view that in an ideal society each person should perform the single task for which he or she is by nature best suited.

Pico, though, was impressed by the variety of human capacities and activities:

upon man, at the moment of his creation, God bestowed seeds pregnant with all possibilities, the germs of every form of life. Whichever of these a man shall cultivate, the same will mature and bear fruit in him. If vegetative, he will become a plant; if sensual, he will become brutish; if rational, he will reveal himself a heavenly being; if intellectual, he will be an angel and the son of God.

Pico even goes on to offer the possibility of a human's becoming one with God:

And if, dissatisfied with the lot of all creatures, he should recollect himself into the center of his own unity, he will there, become one spirit with God, in the solitary darkness of the Father, Who is set above all things, himself transcend all creatures. (*Oration on the Dignity of Man*, 1956: 7–9)

Nevertheless Pico's chief point isn't man's unity with God, but a human being's fundamental plurality, whose attractiveness he doesn't in the least deny: "Who then will not look with awe upon this our chameleon?"

One answer to this question already was, of course, "Plato."

The value that Plato attached to a harmony of aims, as I noted earlier, was attached to diachronic as well as synchronic integration, and accordingly also to prudence. Just as there have been thinkers who were indifferent or hostile to harmony in general, there have of course been those who have the same neutral or negative attitudes toward prudence. For an illustration one can hardly do better than to quote Céline:

Those who talk about the future are scoundrels. It's the present that matters. To evoke posterity is to make a speech to maggots. (*Voyage au bout de la nuit*)

According to this outlook, the idea of an evaluation of one's condition that appeals to one's future states isn't, after all, a "neutral" standpoint, from which one can take all temporal or chronological parts of one's life into account – a way in which one might at 10:00 deal with how one will feel both then and at 6:00, 8:00, and so on. So it's unclear that Céline could ever persuade himself to set his alarm clock (see Chapter 4).

But How to Harmonize?

In spite of the nearly continuous presence of opposing views, most philosophers have tended to accept, to one degree or another, Plato's view that happiness must consist in some kind of harmonization of desires, aims, etc., and that philosophy should try to articulate both what that harmony is and how it enables an overall assessment of a person's condition.

But that hasn't been easy. One of the things that the history of happiness shows is how hard it is.

Plato's own notion of the natural function of each element of the human personality, on which he relied to explain the proper role in well-being that each aim should have, has never lacked advocates from his time to the present. On the other hand many philosophers who have accepted something like that notion have applied it in quite different ways from Plato (Chapter 4).

For example, Freud's scheme of id, ego, and superego is a descendant of Plato's division of the soul into appetite, spirit, and reason, but it's motivated by rather different considerations and issues in quite different recommendations. (Thus Freud doesn't advocate a complete governance of the personality by the superego analogous to Plato's rule of reason.) Even Aristotle's use of the notion of nature and natural function, which in many ways resembles Plato's, is applied very differently and with very different results. Stoic and Epicurean conceptions of nature diverge from Plato's even more. And when Christian ideas enter in, the results are more different still. More recent philosophers – Hume, Kant, and Sidgwick are examples – are skeptical about Plato's or any similar use of the notion of nature in ethics.

But if one thinks that human well-being consists in a harmony of aims of which an account should be possible, but if one rejects the notion of nature or natural function as an explication of it, then what is one to use?

The problem isn't that there aren't enough candidates. Rather, there are too many. And there are too many ways in which they can be applied. Just to convey an impression of what varied options there have been, historically, for someone wanting to select a way of evaluating a person's condition, I'll describe two sets of them. There are more (Chapters 3, 4, 7).

For one thing, a person can take lots of different *perspectives* on his aims and the things that he considers worthwhile or enjoyable. Not only does one think about these things at different times (when one's setting the alarm, when it's ringing, and so on). In addition, one can distinguish between one's desires and pleasures, etc., *as they actually are* and *as they would be if one were fully informed*. Suppose, for instance, that enjoyment is part of one's happiness (as it seems to me obviously to be, even if it's not the whole of happiness). But is my happiness affected by my actual enjoyments, or those that I'd have if I had more experience and could make more comparisons?

Plato took a stand for the latter answer. When he asks how the comparative values of different pleasures are to be determined, he poses the question, "Of the . . . types of men, which has had the most experience of all . . . pleasures?" (*Rep.* 582b), and accepts the verdict that he thinks is delivered by the person who has full experience. A similar thought was applied much later by Hume to issues about taste:

> Where men vary in their judgments [of taste], some defect of perversion in the faculties may commonly be remarked; proceeding either from prejudice, from want of practice, or want of delicacy; and there is just reason for approving one taste, and condemning another. ("Of the standard of taste")

Still later Mill was of much the same opinion:

> Of two pleasures, if there be one to which all or almost all who have experience of both give a decided preference, irrespective of any feeling of moral obligation to prefer it, that is the more desirable pleasure. (*Utilitarianism*, ch. 2)

But an argument has often been made on the other side. Why, one might ask, should whether or not I'm happy be established on the basis of judgments made from a standpoint that I don't or perhaps can't adopt? Why should the fact that I *would* judge such-and-such desirable, if I were in a different state from the one that I'm actually or normally in, mean that such-and-such contributes to my happiness as I am? At best, one might believe, it should contribute to my happiness as I would be, if I *were* in that state, or if I were to change myself so as to be in that state (as perhaps I should do but might not). If I understood cricket, then perhaps watching a cricket match would make me happy; but I don't, so – it seem plausible to argue – it doesn't. Why should a judgment about happiness be any different?

Along a quite different dimension we can also envision – and find in the history of the discussion – different strategies for arriving at the concept of a good or best condition. All of these take as their point of departure features or episodes of life that many people desire, or think are worthwhile or good. That's to be expected, given that the notion of happiness is developed out of aims and considerations that we actually have.

The way that Plato employed was to take all of those aims, desires, pleasures, etc., and apply to them what one might call an organizing filter. A good condition of a person was to be the result of arranging activities and experiences that people actually have. Some of them – those seen as generating avoidable conflicts – would be modified and curtailed, and others would be eliminated. The output of the filter, so to speak, would be a harmonious pattern or combination or structure of the things that made up its input (the chaotic and conflict-ridden set of aims of a person in poor or uneducated condition). The best possible human life would be a life that conformed to such a pattern. This is for the most part Plato's conception, and it's often ascribed to Aristotle as well, at least as the "second-best" life (*NE* X.7–8; Chapter 4).

A very different route to a conception of well-being consists in the identification of it with the extension, so to speak, of what are taken to be the best moments or episodes in a human life. This way of thinking is exemplified by some passages in Plato's *Republic* and *Symposium*, and also in Aristotle's description of what later was called the *vita contemplativa*. It shows itself also in Aquinas' and Augustine's descriptions of, respectively, *beatitudo* and *felicitas*. Thus Aquinas: "perfect human happiness (*beatitudo*) consists in the vision of the divine essence" (*Summa theologica*, IaIIae.5.5); and Augustine:

> The reward of virtue will be God himself, Who gives virtue, and Who has promised Himself to us, than Whom nothing is better or greater. . . . God will be the end of our desires. He will be seen without end, loved without stint, praised without weariness. (*City of God*, XXII.30)

This is a description of the best state experienced by a person, or something analogous to it, extended without limit, not a combination or structure of all good activities and the like.

A third way to deal with the question is typified by certain forms of hedonism, especially *quantitative hedonism*. I'll say more about it later (Chapter 3). What this kind of strategy does is, first of all, to isolate what it claims is that feature of valuable episodes of life that makes them valuable. Quantitative hedonism takes *pleasantness* to be the feature of valuable episodes – namely, experiences – that makes them valuable. It takes this feature as capable of being measured. It then suggests that all experiences can be measured by how much of that feature they have, and value ascribed to them on that basis. The notion of happiness comes in when one says that the higher one's life or condition scores by this measure, the happier one is.

The idea of such a measure can be carried out in different ways. In antiquity it was done in Plato's *Protagoras*, and also by Epicurus. The idea was developed to a substantial degree in the nineteenth century by Bentham (Chapter 3).

These three ways of thinking give quite different answers to the question how well off a given person is. They consider (a) the pattern of a person's various activities, (b) how much he's been in one of a certain set of claimed optimal states (either contemplation, beatitude, pleasure, or whatever), (c) how much of a certain feature (e.g., pleasantness) attaches *in toto* to the periods or moments of his life. These measures aren't equivalent. Someone who scores high in one might well score low in either of the others.

You can't easily say that we just have different standards of evaluation (or scoring systems, if you like), and that it's meaningless to choose among them. Each corresponds to its own view of what's valuable in life and worth seeking. It makes sense to say that a life that conforms to a well-balanced pattern of activities is *happier than*, or *less happy than*, one that doesn't but does contain substantial good episodes, or else a large quantity of pleasure over its whole span. It might appear that a choice of style of evaluating a person's condition has built into it a certain conclusion about which element of happiness is most valuable (see Chapter 7).

Challenges to Happiness

The challenges in question here are challenges to the whole concept of happiness: rejections of a central role for it, and of the idea that it makes sense. They deny that there can be a coherent, understandable such concept, which takes all aims and considerations into account and incorporates them all into a single assessment of a person's condition.

They're of two kinds. One says that there are aims, which are rational aims, that lie outside the concept of happiness, so that happiness can't embrace all aims. On this view, there are rational considerations that compete with happiness to govern a reasonable person's decisions. The most important example of such a consideration would be *morality*. The idea would be that there can be a conflict, in deciding what to do, between one's own happiness and the demands of morality, conceived as something distinct from it.

The other challenges say that (whether or not there are aims lying outside happiness) there is no such concept as happiness because our various aims, etc., simply can't be pulled together into a coherent whole. They thus couldn't be all taken into consideration in forming a single, all-embracing assessment of a person's condition. There would thus be no way of conceiving of such an all-embracing assessment, and no possible philosophical account of it.

It's possible to combine these two ideas. It's possible to maintain both that there are aims, and indeed reasonable aims, that aren't a part of happiness, and also that there's no coherent way of pulling considerations together to form a single evaluation of how good a person's condition is. Kant held this position, or something close to it (Chapter 4).

The other challenge was brought by Gorgias and "Callicles," though not explicitly. In the *Gorgias* Plato doesn't make either of them assert outright that there's no way of bringing all of your desires together and trying to satisfy them as a coherent totality. Instead, he makes them simply ignore this issue, and suppose that happiness is simply satisfying them all one by one, without worrying about whether they conflict. Plato then points out this problem, and says that they have to deal with it.

Thinkers such as Nietzsche don't believe that they should try to deal with it. He in effect denies that there's any way *to* deal with it, since there's no way of bringing together one's aims and taking account of all of them. He doesn't have much of anything to say to people who want self-help instructions about how to be in the kind of condition that he admires. He doesn't really care about the kind of people who want or need such instructions. He himself wouldn't be caught dead trying to give a systematic account of which conflicts are good to have and which one's aren't, or what to do if you're caught in one of the latter.

The view that there's simply no coherent concept of happiness at all is different from the view, discussed earlier, that harmony or consistency of aims is an *undesirable* thing for a person to have. Likewise there's a difference between saying that the concept of happiness is incoherent and that happiness is unimportant. These views are consistent with each other, though, and Nietzsche seems to have held all of them.

Moreover proponents of all of them would deny that a philosopher or thinker ought to give an account of a coherent overall reconciliation of aims – in the one case because it would be unimportant or even bad for a person to make his life conform to such a harmonious scheme, and in the other case because formulating such a scheme is impossible.

So far the assumption has been in force, tacitly, that when we consider what happiness is and which things contribute to it, we're trying to evaluate things so that they all add up to a single judgment about our condition. Departing from this assumption, on the other hand, means rejecting the idea that the evaluation of a person's condition or life is possible in any significant all-inclusive way. That's why I've been discussing the idea of a single point of view from which to assess someone's condition. Much of the history of the philosophical treatment of happiness conforms to the assumption. That's because most philosophical treatments of happiness aspire to present a clear account of a coherent concept.

Kant severed the connection between two kinds of assessments – of moral condition and degree of happiness – more radically than they'd ever been severed before, even though the idea of some separation had already existed as early as Greek times, and many philosophers leading up to Kant had worked on its articulation and clarification (Chapter 5).

On the one side Kant placed the evaluations that attach to the elements of a person's happiness: the things that fulfill a person's desires or, as Kant called them, "inclinations." He placed moral assessments – a good will and the actions that flow from it – on the other side of the distinction.

We can compare this idea to a system of double bookkeeping or double scorekeeping, one column for moral condition and another for other aspects. Whether a person has a morally good will is one thing; whether he's happy is another. The two scores don't combine, on this view, to yield a single overall score, just as you can't subtract the number of penalties against a football team from the number of goals that it scored to get an overall result, which could then be compared meaningfully with the result for the other team. In these terms one can think of Kant as having espoused (with qualifications) a belief in existence of a gulf or "incommensurability" between the two scores.

He also insisted on the superior rationality, clarity, and import-ance of the moral score. In effect he said that there's no clear way of keeping the score associated with the word "happiness," only a vague and uncertain one. It would be a little like drawing a distinction between the number of goals that a team scored with the number of "good plays," and saying that the former number is both more precise and more significant in evaluating the team's success.

The relationship between happiness and morality is important and problematic enough to demand a chapter to itself (Chapter 5). But on its own the idea that there might be more than one scheme of assessment, and no single all-embracing scheme, is significant.

Even if the moral assessment of a person is separated off from the determination of whether he's happy, most thinkers exhibit a strong propensity to contend that the remainder – the aspects that are left over after the moral assessment has been made – must be capable of being pooled together to determine how happy the per-son is. Philosophers after Kant, Schiller and Mill and Sidgwick for instance, thought in this dualist way: one kind of consideration belongs under the label "morality," and the other under "happiness" or "(self-)interest" (though this isn't their terminology).

These thinkers also show an inclination (already referred to in connection with Aristotle and the Judgment Day) to try to think of happiness as being as all-embracing as they can. Most people stick to the idea that even if morality is something separate, all of your other aims and considerations belong together under the heading of your happiness. There's something in most people that makes them want to sum everything in their lives up, if they can.

That propensity, however, isn't irresistible. In addition to morality and perfection (and their combination in the notion of moral perfection), further candidate scores or evaluations can figure as potential rivals to them, and to happiness. Some thinkers would take *beauty* to be one, or even to split up into several different ones. So would sublimity, which has a long history going back to Longinus' treatise *On the Sublime* and beyond, and is something like the grandeur that attracted Nietzsche. *Self-realization* or *self-development* suggest standards of evaluation that can be taken to be either equivalent to happiness, or a part of it, or a rival to it, as when Benjamin Constant says, in his 1816 essay, "It is not to happiness alone, it is to self-development that our destiny calls us" (p. 327). The list might be extended.

Chapter 3

Pleasure, Hedonism, and the Measurement of Happiness

The Idea of a Single Measure

The view that happiness is pleasure – *hedonism* (after the Greek word *hêdonê*, pleasure) – is one of the most widely accepted accounts of what happiness is. In spite of its appeal, it fails for very straightforward reasons. We can learn a lot, though, from its failure. We can learn what we wanted from an account of happiness, and something about what we can't have.

To learn this lesson, the kind of hedonism to concentrate attention on is what's called *quantitative hedonism*. The goal of quantitative hedonism – a worthy goal – is a high degree of systematicity and theoretical power. Fully developed and exploited, it would enable us to measure the value of everything we experience and do, and the extent of its contribution to our happiness.

Nevertheless quantitative hedonism has the defects of its virtues. It's too powerful systematically. It's too powerful to fit the facts that it needs to fit if it's to be convincing. These are the facts about what human beings aim at and value, and even the facts about the things that they enjoy and take pleasure in. These are unsystematic in an inescapable way. Or at least they are so when viewed from the standpoint that philosophers normally take up when they look for an account of happiness. Although being systematic is a virtue of a theory, quantitative hedonism turns out to be too systematic for what philosophers exploring happiness need it to do.

One standpoint from which philosophers normally think about happiness involves deliberation: thinking about what to do or try to do, or try to get or how to be (Chapter 2). Philosophers want to know, that is, what we can consider happiness to be when we deliberate about how to be happy. They want to know this both about how we actually do deliberate, and about how we should deliberate. Incorporated into the thinking that's done from this standpoint, quantitative hedonism about happiness would indicate that we do, and that we should, aim for as much pleasure as possible. But quantitative hedonism doesn't seem up to this demand; it's not believable either as an account of what we do when we deliberate, or as an account of how we ought to deliberate.

Thinking about how we deliberate means thinking about the options and considerations and aims *as they present themselves* to us. The things that present themselves to us are often complicated, but they present themselves to us in pretty simple ways. Shall I take ice cream or cake or fruit salad? Shall I become a doctor or an engineer? For some theoretical purposes, e.g. in economics, it's necessary to think of choices among extremely complex options – "bundles" of goods, as they're called, somewhat analogous to market baskets of groceries.

But ordinary deliberation and much of the philosophy that's done about it focus on – in this analogy – the individual packages of groceries in the basket or bundle. People's minds aren't equipped to think about the value of a bundle of goods except as a function of the values of the goods that make it up. Even the complex options, like becoming a doctor, are presented as simple, and are sometimes compared with things that are much simpler (on the day of the yearly entrance exam for medical school you ask yourself, "Shall I become a doctor or just sleep through the exam?"). This is a limitation on human thinking (sometimes a damaging one). But it determines, nevertheless, the way in which philosophical questions about happiness have been posed throughout the whole history of the concept. It must also determine, most likely, the form that the answers to those questions have to take (Chapter 7).

The fundamental reason why quantitative hedonism isn't convincing in either of these ways goes back to the plurality of our aims and values (Chapters 1 and 2). *As they present themselves* to us, the things that we aim at and the things that we value form an array of different things, which often seem inconsistent with each other. Quantitative hedonism attempts to bring this plurality back to a single thing: quantity of pleasure. The systematic virtues of this kind of systematization are considerable. Nevertheless when we look at this view from anything like our normal standpoint, we see that it claims to find a uniformity in our aims and values that simply doesn't seem to be in them, and that we very probably can't impose on them either.

According to a standard and typical form of quantitative hedonism, roughly formulated, an objective measurement can be made of the amount of pleasure (and of pain, taken as a negative amount of pleasure) that a person experiences at any given moment. Once that's done, the amounts that he experiences at different moments throughout an interval can be added up to give the amount of pleasure over that interval. After that, knowledge of people's reactions could tell us how much pleasure (or pain) would be experienced under different circumstances.

If such an account is right, then it should be applicable to any concrete situation. Then, for example, we might be able to compare the total pleasantness of anything that happened to a person. For instance we could compare the pleasantness of someone's being woken at 6:00 to begin the day, being woken at 8:00, and so on. Armed with this information, the alarm-setter could pick the most pleasant moment at which to set the alarm. Likewise, by applying this strategy to many people simultaneously, the maker of social policy ought to be able to plan to maximize the happiness of a whole society or population, or even all humankind.

It's evident that a hedonism of the sort that's just been described would have to use the word "pleasure" in a broader sense than it has in many colloquial uses. In ordinary contexts "pleasure" often refers simply to particular diversions and also to the enjoyment that comes from eating, drinking, sex, and other such activities. That fact has given hedonism a bad name among those who have moral or similar objections to pleasures of that kind:

> If pleasure is sovereign then not only would the greatest virtues have to be laid low, but in addition it would be hard to say why . . . a wise man shouldn't have very many vices. (Cicero, *De finibus*, II.117)

Hedonists, however, have usually denied that their view is open to such moral objections. Their denial has often been based on the ground that the greatest pleasures, as they see things, come from quite other sorts of things, including altruistic actions, intellectual activities, or simply enjoying a sunny day. At any rate I'll leave moral issues of this sort aside here, and take them up later (Chapter 5).

It's easy to see how quantitative hedonism, if it were true, might be expected to solve most or even all of the problems that arose earlier (Chapter 2). We wondered how to make various comparisons of values, in the face of conflicts between options and different viewpoints on them. The conflicts that I stressed are conflicts of desires and other sorts of aims, intentions, projects, and the like. We can also include pleasures and enjoyments as well, since one kind of pleasure can be impossible to have in conjunction with another, and the activities that we enjoy can be incompatible too.

Quantitative hedonism gives the appearance of providing the solution to these problems. If aims and the like are in question, just take the amount of pleasure associated with each option, and use that to measure its value and its contribution to happiness. (It's hard to say what "associated" means here, but I'm going to assume that the relation is clear enough for present purposes.) If the options are pleasures themselves, then just measure their quantities and compare them. Then pick the option with the highest value according to this measure. In principle, it seems, nothing could be simpler or more compelling.

An Approach to Hedonism in the *Gorgias*

It's unclear whether the positions that Plato's *Gorgias* puts into the mouths of Gorgias and "Callicles" should be described as outright "hedonist." However, they share enough features with views that are plainly hedonist that they're appropriately mentioned here. Moreover they, along with Hobbes's later version of a view much like that of Callicles, raise problems that some undoubted forms of hedonism were designed to meet.

Callicles espouses a policy of satisfying desires as they arise. Sometimes he indicates that doing this would be pleasant, but mainly the emphasis is on simply having the desire and then trying to fulfill it. As Plato says, Callicles doesn't go in much for planning. Desires are mostly to be dealt with as they pop up. The only foresight that Callicles recommends involves putting oneself in a good position to satisfy desires as they occur, and "allowing one's desires to grow as large as possible." He doesn't, however, suggest any very systematic method of desire-gardening or -satisfying. Mostly, to repeat, he recommends just taking desires as they come and satisfying them as you can. Plato demonstrates an unwillingness on his part to stick to this idea (Chapter 2).

In the seventeenth century, Hobbes lays out a related view, though with a complexity that makes it desirable to quote him at length:

> the felicity of this life consisteth not in the repose of a mind satisfied. For there is no such *Finis ultimus* [utmost aim] nor *Summum bonum* [greatest good] as is spoken of in the books of the old moral

philosophers. Nor can a man any more live, whose desires are at an end, than he whose senses and imaginations are at a stand.

Felicity is a continual progress of the desire, from one object to another, the attaining of the former being still but the way to the latter. The cause whereof is that the object of man's desire is not to enjoy once only, and for one instant of time, but to assure forever the way of his future desire. And therefore the voluntary actions and inclinations of all men tend, not only to the procuring, but also to the assuring of a contented life, and differ only in the way; which ariseth partly from the diversity of passions in divers men, and partly from the difference of the knowledge or opinion each one has of the causes which produce the effect desired.

So that . . . I put for a general inclination of all mankind, a perpetual and restless desire of power after power, that ceaseth only in death. And the cause of this is not always that a man hopes for a more intensive delight than he has already attained to, or that he cannot be content with a moderate power, but because he cannot assure the power and means to live well, which he hath present, without the addition of more. (*Leviathan*, ch. 11)

We can see Hobbes as taking Callicles' idea and systematizing it to some extent. That is, Hobbes favors a degree of planning, not the near complete absence of planning that Callicles goes for. Or at least that's so to the extent that Hobbes recommends a policy of trying to gain ever more power, so as to combat likely future dangers to one's satisfaction of one's desires. This isn't too far from what Callicles seems to advocate, but it's spelled out more fully (and connected by Hobbes to much more elaborate views on other, related issues).

Neither Callicles nor Hobbes – no more the latter than the former – has anything to say about the fact that our "perpetual and restless" desires aren't always consistent with each other, or with the constraints of time and the like within which we necessarily operate. Both of them know that our desires encounter obstacles in the world, but neither attends to the fact that those obstacles may be created by the structure, or the lack of it, of a person's desires themselves.

Hedonism in the *Protagoras*

It's precisely this problem that quantitative hedonism was designed to meet, as Plato surely saw when he wrote the *Protagoras*. That work contains the first statement of the position. The things that Plato says there about hedonism probably don't represent his own position, but rather an idea that others had espoused, or possibly an idea that he thought of and simply intends to explore. So in discussing it I'll refer not to "Plato" but to "the *Protagoras*."

The part of the view that earns it the name "hedonism" is:

Doesn't it seem to you ... that these things are bad because of nothing else than that they produce pain and deprive us of other pleasures? (353e–354a)

The part that justifies the word "quantitative" can be seen in this passage:

If you weigh the pleasant against the pleasant, you always have to take the greater and the more; if you weigh the painful against the painful, you have to take the fewer and the smaller. And if you weigh the pleasant against the painful, and if the painful is exceeded by the pleasant – whether the near by the remote or the remote by the near – you have to perform the action in which the pleasant prevails; and on the other hand if the pleasant is exceeded by the painful, then you have to refrain from doing that. (356b–d)

This, says Plato, is an application of what he calls "the art of measurement":

it is by deficiency of knowledge that people err, when they err, in their choice of pleasures and pains, that is to say, of good things and bad things; and from the deficiency not merely of knowledge, but of ... the art of measurement. (357d)

Plato emphasizes the capacity of this measurement to overcome "the power of appearance." "Appearance" makes us mistakenly think that something nearer is larger than something farther away. True measurement, he maintains, has to ignore the influence of spatial perspective. This applies to the measurement of pleasures: one should avoid exaggerating the size of a pleasure that's temporally near. Much later Locke was to express something close to this idea thus:

> the mind having in most cases, as is evident in experience, a power to suspend the execution and satisfaction of any of its desires, and so all, one after another, is at liberty to consider the objects of them; examine them on all sides, and weigh them with others. In this lies the liberty man has: and from the not using of it right comes all that variety of mistakes, errors, and faults which we run into, in the conduct of our lives, and our endeavors after happiness. (*An Essay Concerning Human Understanding*, II.xxi.§47)

Locke's addition here to what Plato says is to point out not only the existence of measurement, but to take note of the "liberty" of a person to apply it.

This "art of measurement" is easily turned into a general strategy for deciding what to do: maximize pleasure (and minimize pain, or displeasure). Even though the phrase isn't used, it's a good label for "always taking the greater and the more" (or, in the case of pains, "the smaller and the less"). For the "maximum" is simply the thing that has a greater quantity of pleasure than any of the others (or the thing that's tied for first place).

One striking fact about the *Protagoras* is the ease with which Plato makes the case for treating pleasure as an object of quantitative measurement and calculation. None of the interlocutors in the dialogue receives the suggestion with surprise. This fact is noteworthy in view of the opposition that quantitative hedonism has sometimes provoked in certain philosophers, who regard it as wrong in the most obvious way. The history of the discussion indicates that quantitative hedonism does indeed turn out to be wrong as an account of happiness. Certainly, though, it has strong initial appeal.

It's striking – also in light of the modern history of quantitative hedonism – that in spite of the naturalness that it strikes the interlocutors in the *Protagoras* as possessing, other works by Plato do almost nothing to elaborate on the idea of measurement of pleasure broached there. *Republic* IX, for its part, makes brief use of the idea that there's a neutral zero-point between pleasure and pain, which is neither the one nor the other. It also says that people sometimes mistake a lessening of pain for an episode of pleasure. Beyond these points there's no further movement in the direction of a more worked-out quantitative scheme, and moreover other works of Plato's express what seems to be a general hostility to hedonism itself.

Aristotelian Pleasure

Aristotle spends a good deal of time discussing pleasure, but what he says is far less systematic than what's in the *Protagoras* (or indeed anywhere else in Plato), and he portrays pleasure as a far less systematically describable thing.

The reason for this isn't so much that he wasn't a hedonist about value and so didn't think that pleasure's the only thing that's valuable, but that he held a particular kind of non-hedonist view about what *is* valuable. As noted earlier (Chapter 2), Aristotle's view is that happiness is excellent activity. He also believed that the relevant kinds of activity are such things as performing ethically virtuous actions and engaging in philosophical thinking (Chapter 4).

On the other hand, although Aristotle doesn't want to maintain straight out that pleasure is happiness, he doesn't want to deny straight out that pleasure is the human good either. He acknowledges the force of the argument that since people and many other creatures seek pleasure, pleasure has a claim to being called their good (*Nicomachean Ethics*, X.1–5). So he doesn't want flatly to say, or flatly to deny, "The good is pleasure" or "Happiness is pleasure." Aristotle's way out of this problem is to say something that sounds extremely paradoxical: that pleasure and (well-engaged-in) activity are *the same*. Here are his words:

> whether we choose life for the sake of pleasure or pleasure for the sake of life is a question we may dismiss for the present. For they seem to be bound up together and not to admit of separation, since without activity pleasure does not arise, and every activity is completed by the attendant pleasure. (*NE* 1175a17–22)

He thinks that this allows him to say that happiness is activity without denying that it's pleasure or at least is very closely tied to it.

Once Aristotle's done this, however, he's barred from treating pleasure in a quantitative or any such systematic way. In his view the varieties and complexities of excellent activity are too great to allow any such thing. Pleasure that's identified with activity, or even tied very closely to it, can't be quantified as it is in the *Protagoras*. Accordingly Aristotle's notion of pleasure is almost completely free of quantitative elements, and subsequent Aristotelian views of pleasure are the same.

Epicurean Hedonism

Epicurus' hedonism doesn't lay claim to being as systematic or, certainly, as mathematically structured as the hedonism hinted at in the *Protagoras*, or as its much later descendant produced by Bentham was to be. But it's quite a lot more systematic and also mathematical than Aristotle's. It also makes far more substantial claims to being usable as a guide to deliberation and action.

According to Epicurus, the good is pleasure. Pleasure is in turn construed as a conscious absence of pain and disturbance. He also maintains that this is what human beings strive for from infancy on, and that in fact people all do strive for it and it alone:

No one rejects, dislikes, or avoids pleasure because it's pleasure, but rather because painful consequences come to those who don't know how to pursue pleasure rationally. (Cicero, *De finibus*, I.32)

This makes it seem that many people, while aiming at pleasure, don't know the best strategy for getting it:

The wise man therefore always holds . . . to this principle of selection: he rejects pleasures in such a way as to secure other greater pleasures, and endures pains in order to avoid worse ones. (Ibid., I.32)

We find in Epicureanism a combination, or perhaps one should say confusion, of two theses that are difficult to disentangle or relate to each other clearly. One – known as *psychological hedonism* – says that everyone does in fact aim only at pleasure as his ultimate end, insofar as he knows how to get it. The other thesis – which we could call *rational hedonism* – says that it's rational for everyone to do so. The former purports to describe how human beings do deliberate; the latter makes a claim about how they should do so.

The two theses aren't equivalent. Moreover, neither implies the other. In particular, philosophers are fond of pointing out that psychological hedonism doesn't imply rational hedonism. That is, that people are a certain way doesn't imply that they should be, or it's rational for them to be that way. If Epicurus took as a premise that people do seek pleasure alone, and inferred from that that people rationally ought to seek pleasure alone, then he was reasoning fallaciously.

Most likely, however, Epicurus believed that since psychological hedonism truly describes people's psychology, there's simply *no point* in urging people to aim at anything other than pleasure, and moreover people have reason to find the best strategy for getting pleasure, since it's all that they ever aim for. An account of happiness that was to be actually *usable* for deliberation by human beings and acceptable to them – as I've said accounts of happiness are normally intended to be – couldn't be inconsistent with their seeking pleasure as their end.

Hedonism and the Measurement of Happiness   51

Although the Epicurean "principle of selection," of "reject[ing] pleasures in such a way as to secure other greater pleasures, and endur[ing] pains in order to avoid worse ones" contains a mathematical component of measurement, the structure that's exemplified is different from the one suggested by the *Protagoras*, and also from the kind of quantitative hedonism espoused by Bentham and others like him. In addition, Epicurus was much less concerned with the measurement of pleasure than with other issues.

On the systematic side, Epicurus appears to have believed that the quantity of pleasure has a *theoretical maximum*. This consists in a complete absence of discomfort and disturbance. According to Cicero, Epicureans deny "that anything can add to the pleasure of someone who is free from pain" (*De finibus*, II.28).

Usually, in fact, Epicurus is reported to have identified pleasure with absence of pain or disturbance (*ataraxia*). This is different from what the *Protagoras* suggests. It also diverges from the contention in Plato's *Republic* (Book IX), that there's a neutral mid-point in our experience, at which neither pleasure nor pain is present. Beyond these statements there's little of importance in Epicurus concerning the measurement and the mathematical structure of pleasure.

On the other hand there's a great deal that Epicurus says from a defensive posture, designed to ward off various objections to a generally hedonist position. This effort has an effect on the themes that he stresses, not just on the style in which he treats them. It leads him away from theoretical questions of measurement, and toward discussions of strategy for obtaining pleasures and not losing them (also common in the types of hedonism found in the eighteenth century).

Epicurus goes to great lengths to say that the kind of pleasure that he favors isn't the kind that either leads to immoral behavior or damages a person's capacity to enjoy further pleasures:

> The pleasure that we pursue is not that kind alone which directly affects our being with delight and is perceived by the senses in an agreeable way. Rather we hold that the greatest pleasure is one that's

experienced as a result of the complete removal of pain. (Cicero, *De finibus*, I.37)

He emphasizes the quiet pleasures, for instance, including the pleasures of friendly company and those of philosophy. But although he talks freely of which pleasures are "greatest," he doesn't have much to offer concerning how such measurements are made. His main point is, given the assumption that they *can* be made, how to gain the greatest pleasure – i.e., the least disturbance – by seeking out those kinds of pleasures that won't be disruptive.

A problematic point for Epicurus was the question why some people actually seem to *reject* hedonism. The question is difficult for him to answer, because on his view everyone does aim at pleasure, always. He can say that most people fail to follow the right strategy to attain it. But on Epicurean grounds it's unclear how a person ever fails to recognize that he's aiming for pleasure, or ever deliberately sacrifices – as people evidently do – pleasure for the sake of some other aim. Seemingly he must say that people must be simply wrong when they say that they strive sometimes for things besides pleasure, or give up pleasure for other things.

The strategy that Epicurus must recommend in order to attain happiness, on his terms, depends on whether he thinks people do ever knowingly aim at anything distinct from pleasure and conflicting with it. If so, then to attain happiness a person would have to have something – reason, acting as a filter – that would put those motivations aside, so that a person would aim at pleasure. But if everyone already does aim only at pleasure, then of course no adjustment is necessary, only a discovery of the right strategy.

Bentham and Systematic Quantitative Hedonism

The advantages of hedonism are two. One – which appeals to almost all theorists to some degree – is that, as Aristotle stressed, it takes happiness to be constituted by something that, however exactly it should be identified, everyone finds attractive, or even attractive in the extreme. It's so attractive, in fact, that virtually every philosopher who's not a hedonist has felt obliged to explain why not. The other advantage – which has appealed to some philosophers but by no means all – is that, as noted, pleasure can plausibly be claimed to be the measure of the value of everything as compared with everything else. As is already maintained in the *Protagoras*, that can seem very valuable if one wants to specify methodically what makes for an overall good condition.

Not until the nineteenth century, however, were the latter possibilities of hedonism extensively exploited. Jeremy Bentham developed quantitative hedonism in his work on legal and social theory. In working out his position, he brought out the systematic potential of hedonism and demonstrated the substantial implications for social policy – if the system could be made to work.

The idea of using systematic hedonism to design social policy wasn't new with Bentham. In rudimentary form it already existed in antiquity. After all, Epicurus had used his hedonism to launch a philosopher's campaign to improve the condition of human beings. He'd done this by opposing his doctrines to traditional Greek religion, and encouraging people to think about how to gain pleasure and avoid pain, and to put aside the fears encouraged by religious mythology. To the same end Epicurus developed his atomist physics, as an antidote mainly to religious and mythological theories of natural phenomena.

The Epicurean poet, Lucretius, took up the role of spokesman for Epicurus' attitude:

> When human life lay miserably on the ground before our eyes, crushed by brutish religion, whose fearful face looked from the sky to threaten mortals, a man of the Greeks [i.e., Epicurus] was the first to dare to raise his human eyes to meet her gaze, the first who stood against her. (*De rerum natura*, Bk 1)

Though Epicureanism was never politically institutionalized, it certainly was advanced with the broad aim of the improvement of the human condition.

Bentham's social project was far more detailed than Epicurus' program ever could have been. It was in the first instance conceived as a legal one: to show how a system of laws ought to be constructed so as to produce the greatest amount of pleasure possible.

He begins by equating happiness with pleasure:

> Mankind is governed by pain and pleasure. . . . It is for them alone to point out what we ought to do, as well as to determine what they shall do. (*Principles of Morals and Legislation*, ch. 1)

He then contends that:

> the happiness of individuals, of whom a community is composed . . . is the end and the sole end which the legislator ought to have in view (ch. 3)

in accordance with

> that principle which approves or disapproves of every action whatsoever, according to the tendency which it appears to have to augment or diminish the happiness of the party whose interest is in question. (ch. 1)

In Bentham's conception of the way in which pleasures are quantifiable the quantity of a pleasure is a function of (within a nicety) its intensity and duration. Thus the more intense a pleasure is and the longer it lasts, the greater it is and the more pleasant the episode of its occurrence can be said to be. Bringing about an increase in happiness, and likewise of the good, becomes a matter of increasing the amount of pleasure, calculated in roughly this way. (For the most part, Bentham's scheme requires us to label a pleasure not with an absolute quantity, like "four hedons," but only a certain sort of comparative quantity.)

Given this kind of information, accordingly we could go on to assert that choosing the overall best available action is a matter of choosing the action that would bring about a greater balance of pleasure over pain than any available alternative would.

This last thought brings us to a point that wasn't investigated at all by ancient writers on pleasure, nor in any serious way by anyone up till Bentham. Talking about the "overall best" action, in Bentham's universalist utilitarian theory, involves not just the happiness of one person, or of just *some* persons, but the happiness of *all* people.

However, because Bentham and Mill say that the right action is the one that produces the greatest happiness of the greatest number of people, they immediately run into a problem. This is labeled the problem of "interpersonal comparisons" of pleasure or (to use Bentham's term) utility.

Such a theory requires determining how the pleasures and displeasures of different people measure up against each other. If we want on these terms to be able to decide, as a matter of social policy, which of us gets the chocolate ice cream and which gets the vanilla, we need to determine whether your pleasure from chocolate is more than mine, and other things like that. Without being able to compare different people's pleasures and displeasures, we can't do this.

Whether we can make these comparisons is controversial. So is the question whether the difficulty of making them counts against Bentham's sort of view. Let's proceed for the moment, however, on the assumption that we can indeed make these comparisons. I'll return to the issue later in this chapter.

If we can make these comparisons, then the power of universalist quantitative hedonism turns out to be impressive. The doctrine says that the value of each state of affairs, or indeed of anything to which we might want to attach value, can be pegged to the quantity of pleasure that it brings or is, and that through this the values of any two states of affairs can be compared with each other, as to which is greater or less. No other evaluation, it says, matters.

If this view's accepted, then it appears that all of the problems about plurality and conflict, raised in the previous chapter, can be swept away at once. At the individual level the naturalness of using pleasure, quantified, as a method of well-being is shown by the utter ease with which the *Protagoras* introduces the whole idea, along with the fact that nothing else is proposed that might possess the same degrees of measurability. If we ask how to settle conflicts of desires, whether experienced at one time or (as in the example of the alarm clock) at different times, then the question is answered by just figuring out how much pleasure arises from each alternative and then comparing them. Happiness is defined in such a way as to yield a procedure for every evaluation that anyone would ever want to make, and, it might appear, every choice that anyone ever faces.

From Antiquity through Bentham

It took a long time, as I've said, for the skeletal quantitative hedonism in Plato's *Protagoras* to reach the point of development that we see in Bentham. What happened along the way?

This story is chiefly a story of what *didn't* happen – what didn't happen, that is, during the whole long stretch of time from Greek antiquity until the nineteenth century. Early in Greek thought, for instance in Democritus, we find the idea that pleasure is the good, and also, especially in the *Protagoras*, the idea that quantity of pleasure can be accurately measured. But even given those two ideas, there was a long wait before anything like Bentham's project of systematization emerged. In the meantime, very little happened. The philosophical discussion of the nature of pleasure, and its uses in ethics, moved sideways.

To be sure, there were some developments with plenty of significance for other philosophical issues besides the ones raised by quantitative hedonism. One of the most interesting of these was Aquinas' effort to evolve a view of pleasure that would combine important Aristotelian ideas about it with his Christian doctrines. This effort involved, in particular, locating the notion of the beatific vision that he identified as the supreme happiness. But Aquinas didn't identify the basis of this happiness as pleasure. Rather, he maintained that we love God *propter se*, because of himself or what he is.

The next few centuries witnessed essentially the same debates over the value of pleasure that had been pursued in antiquity. Just as Epicurus had criticized the Stoics for maintaining that we are attracted to virtue for its own sake Lorenzo Valla, the Renaissance Christian humanist, criticized Aquinas' doctrine, which had become the standard Catholic position, and maintained against it that we love God as the dispenser of heavenly pleasure. It seems fair to think of Valla as essentially an Epicurean, though a Christian one in that he maintained that heavenly pleasure isn't obtainable except through grace.

The focus of philosophical thinking about the notion of pleasure, however, took a new turn in the eighteenth century. In antiquity Epicureans and Stoics had argued for and against hedonism on basically empirical grounds (Chapter 6), but their discussions of this issue weren't fully integrated into any straightforwardly empirical study of human action and motivation. In the eighteenth century the climate changed. Treatments of hedonism then became a part of the gradual but accelerating effort, by Locke, Hume, Smith, and others, to develop an empirical and naturalist treatment of human action and motivation, and in general of all phenomena relevant to ethics and politics.

As noted earlier, Locke made use of an idea like that of Plato's "measurement" of pleasure in the *Protagoras*. Unlike Plato, though, Locke adopted a general hedonist position about what motivates people:

> The pleasure that a man takes in any action or expects as a consequence of it is indeed a good in itself, able and proper to move the will. But the moral rectitude of it considered barely in itself is

not good or evil nor in any way moves the will, but as pleasure and pain either accompanies the action itself or is looked on to be a consequence of it. Which is evident from the punishments and rewards which God has annexed to moral rectitude or pravity as proper motives by the will, which would be needless if moral rectitude were itself good and moral pravity evil. (*Commonplace Book* 1693, quoted in Darwall 1995, p. 40, with original spelling.)

Hutcheson argues on the other side, for the existence of a non-hedonist motivation for virtuous action:

what excites us to these actions which we call virtuous is not an intention to obtain . . . sensible pleasure . . . but an entirely different principle of action from interest or self-love. (*An Inquiry . . .* , Introduction)

Hume is on Hutcheson's side of this issue:

[There is] no real or universal motive for observing the laws of equity, but the very equity and merit of that observance. (*A Treatise of Human Nature*, III.ii.1)

In this debate we hear some pretty close echoes of the debate in Hellenistic times between Epicureans and Stoics.

The outlines of what was to become Bentham's quantitative utilitarian doctrine can be seen before him, but only in rough form. The idea that in general the well-being or happiness of people ought to be strived for had occurred to many thinkers. For instance, Cumberland broached the idea of organizing all morals around the attempt to promote the good of all rational beings:

The greatest benevolence of every rational agent towards all the rest constitutes the happiest state of each and all, so far as depends on their own power, and is necessarily required for their happiness; accordingly the common good will be the supreme law. (*A Treatise of the Laws of Nature*, I.4)

Absent here, however, is the notion of a systematic decision procedure, systematically applied in policy. What hadn't been worked out was what promoting the happiness of these beings would consist in, how to determine what promoted the good more or less than something else, and how one might reconcile opposed appearances of where the greatest good might lie. It appears that no one really got started thinking about these questions in an organized way.

The systematization that Bentham introduced into ethics and the theory of happiness was both a stimulus to and an effect of the growing effort to develop the empirical study of human action, individual and social. It was part of the expansion of natural science in the nineteenth century and the development of social science. Bentham's systematization of the notion of happiness, as identified with pleasure, made it something to be theorized with and about: a tool of the general theory of right action, including social policy, and simultaneously the object of theoretical study.

On the one hand, one might hope to *evaluate* anything by specifying the quantity of pleasure associated with it. In addition, a further thing that one could do was to link happiness and pleasure – taken as one – with the systematic, largely non-evaluative *empirical* study of psychology, including the behavior of human beings and also other animals. This linkage is important enough to require a whole chapter to itself (Chapter 6).

One result of this movement was a strong tendency for the treatments of two kinds of issues, evaluative and empirical, to be viewed together rather than regarded as separate. On the one side there were explicitly evaluative and deliberative issues: happiness, the best condition of a human being, and what to do. On the other side there were questions about how a person's conceptions of his happiness cause or otherwise explain his actions or behavior. These two matters had of course necessarily always been closely connected. However, the rapid development of scientific investigation and theorizing gave the connection a new significance. The simple reason was that the scientific investigation of human psychology and action now loomed so large. Since the ethical questions couldn't be entirely detached from those matters, people's views about the ethical questions were inevitably influenced by scientific developments. Another connection, too, was forged by the systematization promised by quantitative hedonism. It would join ethics not only to natural science but also to what's now broadly known as *social policy*.

Bentham, together with both James Mill and his son John Stuart Mill, spoke out for the capacity of quantitative hedonism to settle what had always been controversial ethical questions, by measuring the quantities of pleasure to be produced by one policy or another. John Stuart Mill puts special emphasis on what he thought was the capacity of this way of thinking to settle ethical questions that had been debated for more than two millennia:

> From the dawn of philosophy, the question concerning the *summum bonum*, or, what is the same thing, concerning the foundation of morality, has been accounted the main problem in speculative thought, has occupied the most gifted intellects and divided them into sects and schools. . . . And after more than two thousand years the same discussions continue . . . and neither thinkers nor mankind at large seem nearer to being unanimous on the subject, than when the youth Socrates listened to the old Protagoras. . . . (*Utilitarianism*, ch. 1)

In a similar way later in the century Henry Sidgwick hoped, though with more modest expectations of success, that by being identified with pleasure construed in this way, the notion of happiness might be put on a scientific basis. If that were done, Sidgwick, Bentham, and Mill thought, the best policy to deal with social questions – that is, the way that would produce the most happiness – could be determined in a way that would be convincing to all. And all three, along with many other utilitarians, hoped and believed that this would enable them to influence society decisively for the better – that is, once again, to achieve a greater quantity of happiness.

Problems in Deliberating about Pleasure

The idea of using quantity of pleasure as a way of assessing a person's condition, and of deliberating about how to improve it, has been argued to be subject to certain additional difficulties. In my opinion these aren't as serious as those to be discussed here. Nevertheless they have an important place in the discussions that have gone on. These difficulties arise when someone attempts to deliberate, consciously, about how to gain as much pleasure as possible. They therefore arise as well – if quantity of pleasure is identified with degree of happiness – for deliberation about how to be as happy as possible. They, or versions of them, have often been adduced by opponents of hedonism.

Sidgwick famously labeled one difficulty in egoistic hedonism the "paradox of hedonism." A closely analogous idea was expressed by Aristotle, who said that it's sometimes easier to attain happiness when one doesn't aim for it directly. Sidgwick formulated his "paradox" this way:

> a rational method of attaining the end at which [egoistic hedonism] aims requires that we should to some extent put it out of sight and not directly aim at it. (*The Methods of Ethics*, p. 136)

Sidgwick's formulation focuses on pleasure; Aristotle's deals with happiness.

The purpose of Sidgwick's use of "paradox" is to show that if the goal is to gain as much pleasure as possible, deliberation about how to do so can get in the way of attaining that goal. That's because of a fact about human beings: they can't readily enjoy themselves when they're thinking about how to enjoy themselves.

As Sidgwick recognized, it's not at all clear that there's any real paradox here. You just have to remember, when you're trying to gain as much pleasure as you can, that there's a cost incurred by thinking about how to do it. But that's not surprising. There are *lots* of costs to be incurred in trying to gain pleasure. Getting somewhere pleasant might, for instance, require you to go out in the rain, thus suffering an unpleasant experience in order to gain more pleasure when you come out of the rain into your destination. That's no paradox.

The so-called "paradox" just indicates, then, that when you undertake to gain as much pleasure as you can, you'd better be aware of the costs of deliberating about it. And so you'd better try to have a strategy that, other things being equal, will require less deliberation. Of course you won't be able to avoid all such costs, just as you won't be able to avoid going out in the rain sometimes. Though the situation contains more complications than can be laid out here, this is an utterly familiar state of affairs. (Think, for instance, of people needing to relax, or to fall asleep; they know that they'd better not think too much about it, if they want to succeed.)

Still, the problem can take hold on a scale that matters. Charles Dickens noticed this. In his novel *Hard Times*, he launched a blistering attack on utilitarianism as it had been espoused by Bentham and James Mill (the father of John Stuart). Dickens accused utilitarians of turning life into a dogged, bleak chase after "utility," because they'd constantly be calculating the costs and consequences of what they proposed to do, in child-rearing, education, art, design, and everything else:

> "Fact, fact, fact!" said the gentleman. . . . "You are to be in all things regulated and governed," said the gentleman, "by fact. We hope to have, before long, a board of fact, composed of commissioners of fact, who will force the people to be a people of fact, and of nothing but fact. You must discard the word Fancy altogether." (*Hard Times*, ch. 2)

Dickens seems to accuse utilitarians, especially Bentham (who does indeed adopt an extremely didactic tone in stating how his legal system will work), of favoring architecture and design that would cause no enjoyment to the eye, but would simply encourage efficient actions that would produce various results. Likewise utilitarians were pictured as advocating education exclusively for "useful" business and trades, and as opposing such enjoyable things as art and literature.

John Stuart Mill believed that Dickens had badly misunderstood utilitarianism. Dickens, he thought, had wrongly taken utilitarians to advocate pursuing, as their end, things that would *lead to* good results but weren't themselves enjoyable. But no, Mill protested, in reality utilitarians advocated taking *happiness* to be one's end. The word "utility," in utilitarian parlance, had been mistakenly taken by Dickens, and by other opponents of Bentham, to designate merely actions leading to something, whereas in fact it designated the happiness that such actions might, if rightly calculated, lead to. So Mill complained:

> A passing remark is all that needs be given to the ignorant blunder of supposing that those who stand up for utility as the test of right and wrong use the term in that restricted and merely colloquial sense in which utility is opposed to pleasure.... Yet the common herd, including the herd of writers ... not only in newspapers ... but in books of weight and pretension, are perpetually falling into this shallow mistake. Having caught up the word utilitarian, while knowing nothing whatever about it but its sound, they habitually express by it the rejection, or the neglect, of pleasure in some of its forms: of beauty, of ornament, or of amusement. (*Utilitarianism*, ch. 2)

Mill endeavors to correct them:

> Those who know anything about the matter are aware that every writer from Epicurus to Bentham who maintained the theory of utility meant by it, not something to be contradistinguished from pleasure, but pleasure itself, together with exemption from pain. (Ibid.)

If Dickens understood utilitarianism to advocate always focusing merely on things that bring about pleasure and never on the pleasure itself, then Mill's complaint was fully justified. And it seems likely enough Dickens did to some extent make that mistake. On the other hand, Dickens was also getting at something else. He was getting at the same point that Sidgwick made under the heading, "the paradox of hedonism."

The point that Dickens was also getting at was simply that time spent deliberating could easily tend, to some extent, to get in the way of enjoyment. So time spent thinking about how to gain pleasure would often be time lost to *having* pleasure, except in those special cases where it's pleasant to think about how to get pleasure (which does sometimes happen). He was accusing hedonists of leading people into a miscalculation, by not recognizing how much enjoyment might be lost to the effort to plan to get it. It's easy to see this point between the lines, at the least, in the pages of *Bleak House* – together with, to be sure, the misunderstanding of which Mill accused Dickens.

In fact, the matter is a special case of a much more general phenomenon, which isn't concerned specially with theorizing or deliberating about pleasure or happiness. The general phenomenon is this: the actual doing of very many activities, and not just enjoying them is hindered by *thinking* – not just about pleasure, or about them, but about anything whatsoever. Philosophers are prone to slip into the assumption that anything that one does is better done if one reflects on how to do it. But as most (other) people know, thinking itself undermines the doing of many things at the same time.

Some Problems for Quantitative Hedonism

Another problem, widely thought to cripple Bentham's project, arose from the so-called "interpersonal comparison of utilities." There was widespread dissatisfaction with Bentham's quantitative notion of the measurement of happiness or pleasure or "utility." Bentham claimed, for instance, that the best action in a given situation is the action that brings about the most pleasure for all people taken together. Difficulty was felt especially to lie with the idea of *comparing* the amounts of pleasure that two different people obtain from the same state of affairs or thing. Nineteenth-century theorists were on the whole satisfied that we could do this. In the twentieth century, however, worries became widespread that it isn't possible to find reliable observable evidence for these comparisons. This problem of interpersonal comparisons was seen as a killing blow to Bentham's theory.

This problem doesn't have to do primarily with questions of value. It's more fundamentally an issue about scientific method, which shows itself most visibly in the philosophy of mind and the philosophy of psychology. It has to do with the question how one can tell what some other person or mind is experiencing. Since pleasure seems to be a subjective experience, how can one person know whether another person is really experiencing it, or how much of it he's experiencing?

How could the hypothesis be excluded, for instance, that two different people behave identically even though one experiences much more pleasure than another? But if that possibility isn't excluded, how can one use the evidence of a person's behavior to reach solid conclusions about how much pleasure or pain he's experiencing? But if one can't reach such conclusions, most of the calculations that utilitarians were interested in would collapse.

This worry was harbored especially by psychologists and economists of a behaviorist or quasi-behaviorist turn of mind. They were especially concerned to gather empirical evidence for their statements. Such problems hadn't bothered Bentham or Mill (even though both were fundamentally empiricists on epistemological matters). The problems did, however, play a prominent role in twentieth-century developments.

The upshot was an effort to find a way of carrying out something like the utilitarian systematization without running foul of such problems about evidence. That meant moving from statements about people's pleasure or happiness to statements that would be more easily open to empirical confirmation.

The notion that was fixed upon was *preference*. Beginning early in the twentieth century it had been made – by Frank Ramsey, John von Neumann, and others – into the core of a powerful technical theory. A person's preferences could be revealed to empirical investigation, it came to be widely held, by the choices that he actually made. For example, you may not be able to tell whether the pleasure that I get from my breakfast cereal is as great as the one that you get from yours, but you can tell which cereals we each prefer to which, and to which other breakfast foods, by observing which ones we pick when given the choice. For reasons of this kind Bentham's quantitative hedonism gave place to this way of thinking by social scientists and many philosophers.

Problems for Systematization, Hedonist and Otherwise

Neither the "paradox of hedonism" nor the problem of interpersonal comparisons of utility constituted the pivotal difficulty for the position that Bentham defended. The most severe obstacles to it lay elsewhere. They had to do with the whole attempt to systematize human aims under a concept of happiness. This systematization seems on the one hand to be called for. It seems necessary in order to avoid the deliberative fragmentation and the conflicts that present themselves to us. On the other hand the product of it never fits comfortably – that is, comfortably enough to allow it to be generally accepted – with the aims that we hold to.

Neither quantitative hedonism nor the application of the notion of preference avoid this problem. Consider the latter first.

The notion of preference on its own or merely as it's standardly figured in the theory of choice, wasn't really constructed for the purpose of explicating happiness in the way that philosophers traditionally tried to do. The theory of choice tells us something important about the *structure* of a set of preferences. It tells us such things as this: that a preference ordering of options that's to count as rational by its standard can't be "intransitive." For example, one can't rationally prefer A to B and B to C but prefer C to A, no matter what A, B, and C are. Thus one can't rationally prefer coffee to tea and tea to orange juice but then prefer orange juice to coffee. But nothing in the theory of choice even tried to tell someone, starting from scratch so to speak, whether it's rational to prefer coffee to tea or tea to coffee or to be indifferent between them. Nor – and this is crucial – does it try to tell a person, on its own, whether to prefer coffee and orange juice to tea, or orange juice to coffee and tea.

The traditional purpose of theories about happiness, however, has been to answer questions something like the last one. For that task, once again, has been to take the whole array of our aims and deal with the fact of their large variety (too large all to be satisfied easily together) and the conflicts among them, to take them all duly into consideration, and then to show how the fulfillment of the resulting aims might be construed, all together, as constituting happiness. The aims that come to us for consideration, however, normally have a quite simple structure. Moreover, they don't usually come to us ordered as to preference. They're things analogous (in this example) to: coffee, tea, orange juice, especially if we can't have them all. Our problem is to put all of these relatively non-complex aims (presumably with some thrown out or pruned down) into one grand aim, happiness – *if* that can be done! – and to use it to assess how good a given person's condition is or has been overall (see Chapter 7).

The theory of choice and its component notion of preference never were designed to solve this problem. Such a theory takes a preference ordering (defined from pairwise preferences) for granted, as undefined. It doesn't tell you how to put simpler aims together (whether ordered by preference or not) to get compound or complex ones. It doesn't try to tell you how to get bundles of goods out of simpler goods. This isn't a criticism of the theory of choice (or of the notion of rationality that it proposes to explicate) – only a fact about the domain that it deals with.

A notion of preference, however, has been enlisted by some philosophers in the twentieth century to try to explain what happiness is. The general idea is that well-being consists in the satisfaction of preferences, or "preference-satisfaction." One normal picture is that

if you have a preference ordering of states of affairs from most preferred on down, then the higher up on the scale the actual state of
affairs is, the happier you are.

So far so good, but that doesn't tell you how to construct the
ordering, and especially, once again, it doesn't tell you how – given
the relatively non-complex preferences that present themselves to
you as you consider what you aim for and which of your aims you
put most stock in – to put your simpler aims together so as to make
them, in some sense or other, fit each other.

Obviously the idea that happiness is preference-satisfaction is a
new version – fortified by modern work on the notion of preference
– of Gorgias' idea that "the greatest good" is "fulfilling your desires."
Just as the problem there could be summed up by the question,
"Which desires?," here the problem can be summed up by the question, "Which preferences?" (Chapter 2). Just like your "wants," your
"preferences" as you can identify them in normal life don't fit
together. Fitting them together, or at least saying schematically (not
necessarily in concrete detail) how to do so, is the whole question of
what happiness consists in. Saying that well-being is preference-
satisfaction doesn't answer that particular question.

The twentieth century has seen numerous proposals by
philosophers to try to support the idea that happiness is preference-
satisfaction. One suggestion is that happiness is satisfaction, not of
the preferences that you actually have, but of your fully informed
preferences, i.e., your preferences as they would be if you were fully
informed. This proposal is open to serious objections (though detailed treatment of them is out of place here). However, it can be
hoped that your fully informed preferences would no longer be in
conflict, and would contain just the preferences that can be dealt
with in the span of life that you have available to you. But the problem was to say which those are (or how they can be combined into
more complex preferences). This suggestion – aside from other difficulties – doesn't try to answer that question. For it doesn't tell us
which way of organizing our simple preferences would be provided
by full information.

Lurking behind the various objections to quantitative hedonism and accounts of happiness in terms of preference there's a general source of opposition. The opposition has arisen essentially to the kind of systematization (recently the cliché has been "reduction," but it isn't fully à propos) that they represent. Its target is diffuse, but it includes accounts of happiness as preference-satisfaction (to be clearly distinguished, I stress once again, from the use of the notion of preference in the theory of choice itself), as well as quantitative hedonism, and indeed hedonist accounts of happiness in general.

The best illustration of this generalized opposition can be found in objections to quantitative hedonism. So I focus mainly on that.

Doubts about Bentham's quantitative hedonism arose early in the ranks of utilitarians. As noted earlier, Bentham held that the only factors to affect the quantity of a pleasure are intensity and duration. He also held, notoriously, that if the quantities of pleasure derived from pushpin (the contemporary equivalent of pinball machines) is equal to that from poetry, then the one is just as good as the other, and likewise a noble action is, on those same terms, just as good as a sadistic one (though of course the pleasures associated with their subsequent consequences might make a further difference). That means that the value of an event or experience, for instance, is purely a function of the intensity and duration of the pleasure associated with it (not that this "association" is easy to define).

Mill, though a follower of Bentham, recoiled from this outlook. In Mill's view, pleasures can differ not only in quantity but also in what Mill called "quality." For instance, Mill maintained that even if the intensity and duration of altruistic and sadistic pleasures were equal, the former differs from the latter in quality and also, therefore, in value. "It would be absurd," says Mill,

> that while, in estimating all other things, quality is considered as well as quantity, the estimation of pleasures should be supposed to depend on quantity alone. (*Utilitarianism*, ch. 2)

This is clearly a change from Bentham's doctrine.

It was never quite clear, though, just what Mill thought a difference in quality consists in. However, he certainly believed that differences in the quality of pleasures make a difference to their value. Plainly he wanted to avoid saying that if a sadistic act gives a sadist a great deal of pleasure, it's thereby made valuable. He would have been *required* to say this, however, if he'd stuck to a purely hedonist standard such as Bentham recommended. In effect, then, Mill chooses to depart from that standard (as many critics recognized), and allow his evaluations to be guided by considerations that aren't intrinsic to pleasure itself.

The dilemma that Mill faces here is symptomatic, I think, of the second problem with hedonism that I mentioned just now. The evaluations that most people are willing to accept just don't line up with the quantities of pleasure, in any usual sense, that attach to the things being evaluated. It seems plausible, unfortunately, that sadists receive intense pleasure from sadistic actions, in a sense of the term "pleasure" that we can all understand. Even so, we're like Mill in being simply unprepared to say that that pleasure experienced by the sadist is a good thing, quite apart from any consideration of its quantity.

Mill's objection is an objection to saying that the *degree of value* of something – the degree of its contribution to one's overall happiness – could possibly be a function solely and simply of *how much pleasure* it supplies.

In addition, however, there has been another source of skepticism about quantitative hedonism. It's directed at the idea that, if we put questions about value entirely aside for the moment, it's possible to conceive a complete scale on which we can say *how pleasant* something is.

Although many experiences that are plainly pleasures and displeasures, for instance, do line up together on a scale of more and less, very many of them simply don't. There are, after all, numerous examples of pleasures which it seems very strained to compare with each other along any sort of scale. This frequently happens when the pleasures belong in some sense to different domains which we don't ordinarily think about together. Often, furthermore, pleasures line up on several different scales that can't be integrated with each other except in the most implausible and forced way.

It's hard, for instance, to say which is more pleasant, a fine concert, a warm shower (or nine or ten warm showers), being complimented three times on a nice shirt, hearing a good joke and then remembering it several times, a turn of the weather from intolerably muggy to fresh and only mildly warm – even though these items don't belong to very widely separated domains. Displeasures are hard to compare too. Which is worse, an execrable concert that one has to drive miles to hear, or an execrable meal in an expensive restaurant? It's easy for anyone to construct conundrums of this kind, especially comparing widely differing things.

Such difficulties are common enough to undermine, at least in most people's mind, the thesis that all pleasures can be ranged on a quantitative scale of pleasantness. The notion of quantitative comparisons of pleasure applies well enough to a wide range of cases, but only so long as we don't demand too much precision.

And of course if there are quite a lot of pleasures that we can't range on such a scale, then we can't use the scale to measure the size of a thing's contribution to happiness by how much pleasure it provides.

Mill's reservations about quantitative hedonism, though, aren't just reservations about quantitative hedonism, but about hedonism in general. They don't cast doubt merely on the view that the contribution that a thing makes to someone's happiness always has to do with a *quantity* of pleasure. They cast doubt on the idea that the value of a thing *always* has something to do with pleasure. Certainly this view has continued to be fairly common among philosophers. Moreover Mill says things that many take irresistibly to suggest that he concurs, including his famous saying, "It is better to be a human being dissatisfied than a pig satisfied; better to be Socrates dissatisfied than a fool satisfied" (*Utilitarianism*, ch. 2).

Mill tries to hold that in spite of this, Socrates is happier than the fool (and that those who deny it are confusing happiness with contentment). It's appeared to many plausible, however, that in Mill's statement, "better" doesn't really mean "more pleasant" at all. Rather, Mill is judging value in a way that has nothing to do with pleasure.

It's therefore hard not to understand Mill as shifting away from hedonism and back into an Aristotelian view, according to which pleasantness isn't the main source or bearer of value, but instead the ethical character of the action or even of the pleasure itself:

> Since activities differ in respect of goodness and badness, and since some are choiceworthy and others are to be avoided and still others are neutral, so too are the pleasures, since there's a proper pleasure for each activity. The pleasure proper to a worthy activity is good, and the pleasure proper to an unworthy activity is bad. (Aristotle, *NE* 1175b24–9)

and

> There's nothing surprising if things that the good man finds unpleasant seem pleasant to some people. . . . [T]hese things *aren't* pleasant, but only pleasant *to* these people and *to* people in such a condition. Those that are admittedly disgraceful obviously shouldn't be said to *be* pleasure, except to a perverted taste. (1176a19–23)

Once a significant role, in determining the value of an aim or other part of life and in judging its contribution to overall happiness, has been granted to something other than quantity of pleasure, then a previously systematic scheme is in danger of losing its systematic character. And with that character the scheme is in danger, likewise, of ceasing to provide a clear measure of well-being. That certainly happened to Mill's utilitarianism, as was widely recognized.

By the beginning of the twentieth century, optimism about the utilitarian "calculus" had largely worn off. Sidgwick, though a utilitarian, was frank about the difficulties attaching to the view. He was particularly frank about how hard it is to measure quantities of pleasure actually experienced by human beings. After an examination of the issue, he was willing to conclude:

> I am willing to hope that [a scientific] refuge from the difficulties of empirical hedonism may some time or other be open to us; but I cannot perceive that it is at present [this was in 1907] available to us. (*The Methods of Ethics*, p. 178)

It appears that the grounds for hope have dwindled in the time since Sidgwick wrote, though certainly utilitarianism has remained a source of hope and inspiration for some philosophers to the present day. By now, though, many philosophers have become yet more discouraged than Sidgwick sounded in 1907. The business of measuring quantities of pleasure, and measuring value by pleasure, is by now recognized to be problematic. It doesn't seem at all easy to square with the pre-systematic and non-systematic way in which we view our aims and their relations to each other, which aren't easily caught by a tractable schema or calculus.

The systematic philosopher may well complain. "What do you want from us?," he might well ask. "You complain about the difficulties of coordinating a person's everyday profusion of aims, which so often conflict with each other; and so you ask for a system that will coordinate them; but then when we systematically minded philosophers propose a calculus to you – or at least a sketch of how one might be developed – you complain that it doesn't fit your pre-systematic aims as they presented themselves to you in the first place!" He could go on, "Which do you want? A systematic way of deliberating? Or fidelity to the way in which aims and considerations present themselves to you in everyday life?"

Many people would reply, "Both!" Now we can examine a philosophical tradition that attempts to deliver this.

Chapter 4

Happiness as Structure and Harmony

Outline: the Development of Dynamic Structure

Parallel to the long history of hedonist methods of articulating the idea of happiness, another way of attacking the problem has also been pursued over the same period, from antiquity to the present. Proponents of the two strategies argued against each other over the whole time.

At the end of the previous chapter I noted that a fair number of philosophers decline to accept the ways of coordinating aims that hedonism proposes. Plato and the broad and heterogeneous tradition that follows him offer what looks to be an alternative.

Quantitative hedonism seeks to find, in all of the aims, etc., that we have in ordinary consciousness, a single feature, pleasantness, that's held to carry the value of each of them. Quantitative hedonism then asserts that this feature can be measured, and that the resulting quantities are mathematically comparable, that they can be added together, and so on.

The crucial first step, though, is to find the common feature of all of our aims, satisfactions, and the rest, which provides their value. The conclusion is, in effect, that there really aren't any conflicts between different values, because there's only one valuable feature:

amount of pleasure or degree of pleasantness. The only sources of error would be a failure to measure the pleasantness of something accurately, or a mistake of calculation. These mistakes avoided, actions simply have to be adjusted so as to make this amount as great as possible.

In Plato's view things are quite different. According to him, we can't get away from the idea that to keep aims from conflicting, a certain more complex structure is required than the kind of quantitative scheme that's up for consideration in the *Protagoras*. The required structure has to do more than simply ascribe quantities to various elements of a person's life and to add the quantities up. The idea is that (intuitively) order – structure – matters. C. I. Lewis gives an illustrative example of a closely related kind of non-additivity:

> One could not . . . by selecting from amongst Beethoven's symphonies the three movements which are rated highest, and juxtaposing these, create a better symphony than Beethoven ever wrote. (1946: 496)

Rather, there are various different kinds of desires and satisfactions, which Plato arranges in three classes, those of reason, "spirit" (something close to a sense of one's own dignity), and appetite. Most of these desires tend to conflict with each other. What can keep them from doing so – what can keep them in harmony – is their being *organized* in a certain way. Plato's problem is to figure out what this structure might be, and how a person's personality might conform to it.

Plato thinks that the appropriate style of organization needs a structural description, which would be rather more like a kind of geometry than an arithmetic. He thinks that the best organization of a person's aims is given by considering the "parts" or constituents into which the personality (or "soul," *psyche*) is divided. He usually thinks of these "parts" as the various different desires and motivations that a person has.

Roughly, he believes, the best structure consists in the performance by each constituent of an individual's personality of its *natural function* or task. For example, hunger provides food for the health of the body; the spirit defends the person and his proper sphere of activity; reason coordinates and directs the person's activities overall. That illustrates the kind of structure that Plato has in mind.

By inducing one's personality to conform to this structure, one's reason acts to filter and shape the various aims and other motivations, as well as experiences, to which one is subject. Plato sometimes uses the metaphor of the pruning of a tree or other plant. Reason selects those elements that fit into this pattern of natural functions, and it also reduces and sometimes augments some of those elements – notably the "physical appetites" – so that they fit into it. Instead of the picture of measurement of a common feature, as in quantitative hedonism, we have the picture of a filtering and structuring administered by one part of the personality.

A good many philosophers, e.g., Cumberland and Butler, have found this scheme for organizing a person's aims much more plausible than a quantitative hedonist strategy, or indeed any hedonist view. It seems to them to have the same intuitive character as the idea (even now, with modern biology) that the parts of our bodies have functions: the heart is for pumping blood, the lungs are for absorbing oxygen, and so on.

Although the results of such lines of thought may not coincide with the unsystematic way in which our aims present themselves to us prior to philosophical examination, it's easy for quite a lot of people to feel that this idea represents something that we actually *find in* our personalities, rather than an artificial schematism forced upon it – which is what quantitative hedonism strikes many people as being.

When a quantitative hedonists suggests that you measure the amounts of pleasure that you get from fulfilling various aims, and then calculate which one's greatest so as to decide what to do, many people have the feeling that this doesn't *fit*, so to speak, with the way in which they think about the considerations that should be taken into account. On the other hand, when Plato proposes that each motivation or aim has a function, and that the good condition of the person consists in the performance of function by all elements, people have a sense that this describes something with which they're already familiar. Moreover it can seem believable that the personality is designed in such way that if each motivational part "does its job," the result will be integrated and consistent, with each constituent making its contribution to the good of the whole. Platonists capitalize on this plausibility by suggesting that the personality is, in its good state, an "organic whole."

In spite of this intuitive appeal, however, merely to talk of "structure," or "organization," or "harmony" doesn't really tell us enough about what kind of structure is called for. The notion of structure, whether or not it's supplemented by the notion of natural function, brings substantial obscurities. Most importantly, it seems easy to find many different structures that might be treated as good. Moreover it's often plausible to ascribe more than one function to a given element of the human personality (however those elements be individuated). In that case we have various different ways of structuring the plurality of human aims, etc. We'd need to say something further about which among them is best.

It shouldn't be forgotten that not all philosophers have believed that harmony of aims is to be sought or welcomed (see Chapter 2). Nietzsche is the best example. Perhaps one should say that he's even against structure altogether, not just against harmonious and conflict-free structure. At any rate, he certainly doesn't think that the best life makes up a *harmonious* pattern in any normal sense. And he doesn't think it can be specified in any recognizable way. (It's true enough that if one uses the term "structure" broadly enough, any array can be described as a structure. We're operating here with a more stringent notion of structure or organization, which is intuitively clear in many of the relevant cases, and which allows us to distinguish between an array that's "organized" and one that's "disorganized.")

The attempts throughout history to articulate explicitly an idea of structure haven't, in most respects, produced any very noteworthy increase in clarity of the notion or the guidance that it's capable of providing. That's partly because this tradition in the history of happiness hasn't aimed for that much precision. It hasn't shown, for instance, the exuberant mathematical ambitions of quantitative hedonism. But on the other hand it hasn't suffered the same straightforward setbacks either.

One therefore can easily retain – and not be readily disabused of – the feeling that there's *something* right about Plato's idea. The elements of an individual's personality seem to need to be filtered and adjusted so as to become integrated or harmonized or structured, even if one can't say very concretely what this involves. In most of the time since Plato it seems that, in spite of some attempts (e.g., by Freud), the content of the idea hasn't been specified much beyond this point – if, indeed, it can be (Chapter 7).

Since the ideas falling into this tradition aren't guided by a crisply systematic idea, they've formed a philosophical miscellany, and the following descriptions of them will do the same. I'll lay out some of the main suggestions, and indicate what I think have been the most promising directions for thoughts along these lines.

If there's to be a structure of aims and so on, it needs to be a dynamic structure, not merely a static one. Plato's notion of structure is in an important way static, and the same seems to be true of other ideas that have been developed along the same lines as his.

Ancient ideas about the structure of a person's aims didn't fail to take note of the fact that a life involves change and even development. It's true that Plato tended sometimes to think of "form" as static shape – like the shape of a triangle or a circle or a sphere – although he also believed in kinetic structure too (notably, the pattern of stellar and planetary motions).

Aristotle, though, emphatically conceived of the "form" (as contrasted with "matter") of a living thing as containing within it the development of that thing from infancy to adulthood and then to decay and death. He accords the adult specimen privilege as the true representative of the form of the organism. Nevertheless the form includes movements and activities, such as locomotion, nutrition, and the like. Moreover Aristotle's conception of practical philosophy is a conception of deliberation for action, not just for reaching and occupying a certain static state of being.

Despite that, in a certain sense such views – the Greek views and the many views that stay close to them – of the structure of a person's aims is static after all. Roughly the point is this. The shape of a person's life and activities is thought of as being specifiable in one fell swoop, and in advance. It involved things like a single choice of an occupation (statesman, philosopher, etc.) or of a single end in life (money, fame, virtue). A choice of this sort doesn't settle, of course, all of the details of the actions that will be required to carry it out. However, in Greek and most other philosophers' descriptions of the structure of a happy life, no attention was paid to the idea that the structure of a happy life might need to leave certain alternatives open, to be settled later, perhaps with abstract routines for filling in the unsettled parts as one goes along.

The way in which this is particularly true of Greek philosophy can be explained by reference to the fact that Plato and Aristotle were fundamentally – to use a modern term – "educators." Both of them had schools, and they were in the business of persuading Athenian gentlemen to send their sons to them for training for a career. Consistently with this situation, Plato and Aristotle tended to think that one should be able to lay down a plan for a person's life, which education would enable him to carry out. If the education were successful, then the rest of life could be seen as the implementation of that plan.

In contrast to this view, a person's life can be seen as partly unplanned, or at most with a plan that's essentially open or revisable. This idea comes to the fore only in the nineteenth century, at the earliest. It accepts that a person's aims, values, and enjoyments change and evolve, and that a plan for them has to be indeterminate in important ways, and can be altered as one goes along.

Platonic Structures of Harmony and Nature

One of the earliest recorded ideas about the way in which the activities and aims of a male Athenian might be structured comes from Solon:

> In seven years a young boy casts off the teeth that he cut as an infant. When the god has accomplished seven more years for him he shows the signs of his youthful prime. In the third seven, his limbs grow and his skin changes and his chin grows fuzzy. In the fourth, he has much the greatest strength, which men take as a sign of excellence. In the fifth seven, it's time for a man to give thought to marriage and to leave children as offspring to come after him. In the sixth, his mind is trained in all things, and he doesn't strive to do things that can't be done. In the seventh seven both his mind and his tongue are by far the best, and also in the eighth – fourteen years for the two. He's still able in the ninth, but his tongue and his intelligence are less powerfully excellent. If a man arrive at the end of the tenth seven, it won't be untimely for him to meet his fated death. (fragment 27)

This passage suggests that we plan our lives, in a sense, but that we plan it in accordance with some fixed facts about how it's going to go. Mostly, it tells us what we have to expect, if we're lucky, whether we like it or not. The natural course of life takes care of much of our planning for us. At certain ages a male is ready for certain things; at others, for others.

Some of this way of thinking shows up at the beginning of Plato's *Republic*, in the person of the old man, Cephalus. He's prepared for aging to take its course, but he doesn't think that a person's own actions are without influence on his condition:

When the appetites ease off and stop pressing us . . . we escape from many insane masters. In these matters . . . the real cause isn't old age, but the way people live. If they're moderate and contented, old age is only moderately burdensome; but if they aren't, then both old age and also youth are hard to bear. (329c–d)

Plato, it's already emerged (Chapter 2), thinks that for a life to go well more intervention by reason is necessary. Otherwise various desires will thwart each other and bad ones will take control. If a person's reason is able, he can organize his own activities. Otherwise, he has to be "controlled from outside," by force and punishments.

We should distinguish between two aspects of the Platonic view of harmony of the personality: the formal and the substantive.

The *formal* aspect tells us very little more than that reason should rule. That says relatively little that's concrete. It does take for granted that aims need organizing, because otherwise they'll get in each other's way. It then says simply that the personality should be organized by the aspect of it that possesses the capacity to organize it.

The *substantive* aspect of Plato's view tells us, more concretely, that reason is the part that engages in rationalist philosophy, and seeks from it guidance as to how to organize one's aims. This aspect also tells us that the bodily appetites are disruptive and should be controlled. It tells us, too, that a kind of courageous self-respect (located in what Plato calls the "spirit") plays a part in helping one control the appetites, because it makes one feel ashamed at a loss of self-control.

By the end of Plato's exposition, both formal and substantive aspects of his account combine. Together they present a fairly detailed portrait of a person who's in what is supposedly the best possible human condition. This person is intellectually disposed and accomplished, but also well trained for athletics and military activity, schooled in music and dance, and prepared by his or her philosophical understanding to take charge of society. This portrait gives us far more than the bare idea of a coordination of aims to keep them from clashing. It shows us a very particular manner of trying to coordinate them.

What does Plato tell us about how reason is to organize one's personality? His description of the necessary structure is to some extent metaphorical. A good man, as we've seen him saying,

> doesn't allow any part of himself to do the work of another part, or the various elements in him interfere with each other. He organizes what's really his own well, and rules himself. He puts himself in order, is his own friend, and harmonizes the . . . parts of himself like . . . limiting notes in a musical chord. He binds those parts together, and any others in between, and from having been many he becomes entirely one, moderate and harmonious. (443d)

This is an evocative description, but neither a precise one nor a clear guide in and of itself. It's not even a full enough description to show that what Plato thinks should be done really can be done.

One idea that bears much of the weight of Plato's suggestion is, of course, this: each element of the personality has a natural role or task to perform within the economy of the whole. Another is that these natural tasks don't themselves clash with each other, so that when they're performed the person is harmonious. That incorporates what could be called an optimistic view of "nature." It reflects Plato's belief, expounded in his *Timaeus*, in the organizing presence of intelligence in the cosmos as a whole.

Another component of Plato's view is the idea that not only should reason organize the personality and also the ideal city-state, if the person lives in one, but it also should engage in the necessary philosophical thinking to enable this to happen. So there's a residual conflict between two aims of the philosopher-ruler, since one can't engage in philosophy and politics simultaneously. Reason thus has two distinct natural tasks. Here we have what was historically to be a standing question about the compatibility of the *vita activa* and the *vita contemplativa*.

Philosophers influenced by Plato – strongly enough so to believe that the best condition of a human being is a kind of harmony or integration of the personality – have often seen a difficulty in Plato's particular application of the idea that each element of the personality has a natural task.

Plato seems to be of the opinion that in order to be able to see to this integration of oneself, a person must have a full philosophical training, including a full philosophical understanding of the concept of the good (*Republic*, VII). "Why so?," many have asked. Why shouldn't there be, short of this, a level of practical understanding that's fully sufficient for wise management of oneself?

Aristotle raised the same question. His response was that a person with practical intelligence doesn't have to be a philosopher and doesn't have to engage in philosophical contemplation (*Nicomachean Ethics*, X.6–8). Most people have likewise believed that full philosophical understanding itself is to some extent a specialized affair, which only certain people need to engage in, and which most people can get along without, and still attain the happiness that they're capable of without the direction of philosophers.

What does Plato think is so desirable about the sort of harmonious condition that he recommends? As I've said (Chapter 2), he has three reasons for thinking that an absence of harmony is bad. Lack of harmony entails frustration of some aims; it shows that some parts of the personality aren't performing their natural functions; and it manifests a kind of irrationality: in particular, a failure of reason to have a clear notion of the consistency of the character.

Corresponding to each of these bad features of disharmony, there is in Plato's view something desirable about harmony. There's unimpeded satisfaction, the realization of each part of the person by its performing of its own function, and also, it seems, an enjoyment of harmony *per se* by the reason.

This last idea was emphasized by many philosophers in the Platonic tradition, and often was linked to Christian theology. It was important in the Neoplatonic tradition, notably in the Renaissance.

The idea crops up, for instance, in Pico della Mirandola's *Oration on the Dignity of Man*:

> If, by moral philosophy, the power of our passions shall have been restrained by proper controls so that they achieve harmonious accord; and if, by dialectic, our reason shall have progressed by an ordered advance, then, smitten by the frenzy of the Muses, we shall hear the heavenly harmony with the inward ears of the spirit. Then the leader of the Muses, Bacchus, revealing to us in our moments of philosophy, through his mysteries, that is, the visible signs of nature, the invisible things of God, will make us drunk with the richness of the house of God; and there, if, like Moses, we shall prove entirely faithful, most sacred theology will supervene to inspire us with re-doubled ecstasy. (pp. 26–7)

Pico may be thinking of the ecstasy as something over and above the gratification experienced by the reasoning part of the soul when its desires are satisfied without interference, an experience that arises from the harmony itself overall and not from any single component satisfaction within it. (After all, on the other side of the issue Nietzsche appears to think that a similar exhilaration can be produced by psychological conflict.)

Although Plato contends that the direction of the personality by reason is a kind of harmony of a person's aims and enjoyments, it doesn't appear that everyone can be in this condition. Not everyone, he believes, has a reason that's capable of ordering his personality effectively. People in whom reason doesn't organize the other desires aren't *on their own* harmonious in this way. *Republic* IX explicitly states that in the ideal city, such people have to be governed by reason "from outside," i.e., the rulers will have to control them by means of punishments. Likewise people being educated to play the role of guardians in the ideal city are explicitly said to be in need of external control.

In addition, it's somewhat obscure to what extent Plato really intends to ascribe even to the fully educated philosopher-rulers a condition that's entirely harmonious, without any oppositions at all. This is a disputed interpretative point. It may be that even in the best-endowed and best-trained philosophical personality, in Plato's view, desires do remain that are recalcitrant to reason, and have to undergo continual training or control. On the other hand, one remark that Plato makes in the last book of the *Republic* may be intended to suggest that only when the soul is released from the body by death might it show itself to be entirely unitary:

> Then we'd see what it's real nature is, and be able to tell whether it has many parts or just one, and whether or in what manner it's put together. (612a)

In any case, Plato does seem to be committed to this: the more harmony, and even unity, the better.

According to Plato, an ideal ruler's reason should organize and harmonize not only his or her personality, but also the city-state or *polis*. One particular aspect of this parallel is especially germane to the notion of happiness.

In Plato's opinion, these two activities resemble each other in requiring, each of them, that a ruler eschew the satisfaction of current desires that demand present satisfaction – Plato focuses on what he calls bodily desires. The problem is posed in the *Gorgias* by Gorgias and Callicles (see Chapter 2), and subsequently by Aristippus and others (such as, in effect, Hobbes). Suppose that one currently has a desire that some state of affairs obtain immediately, for example, to eat. The question seems to arise: what motivation might present itself that would persuade one to forgo satisfaction of that desire and to strive here and now for something else instead?

This question can arise equally whether the "something else" is an action conducive to the satisfaction of some desire of one's own in the future – perhaps of the same kind as one's present desire – or to the satisfaction of a desire of someone else, or to something like the organization of one's society. Plato treats all of these cases as analogous to each other. He also tries to respond to the question that they raise in essentially the same way.

Plato's strategy is to suppose that in general the reason is repelled by contradiction or conflict or disorder (all of these being taken together as closely similar phenomena), and loves and seeks to bring about the opposite, consistency or harmony or order. The order in question is: for each part of a complex entity to perform its natural function (and not to perform the natural function of any other part).

The function of reason is to rule, and so in a well-ordered personality – i.e., in a personality in which each part performs its natural function – reason will seek to maintain this state of affairs in the personality of which it's a part. In a well-organized society it will seek to maintain, likewise, the order of the society in which it is. Plato maintains that such a personality and such a society is happy. The important point is that a person's reason has exactly the same interest in the harmony of that person as it does in the harmony of his society: the performance of natural function by each functional part of a personality or a society. In modern terms, prudential motivation and moral and altruistic motivation are essentially the same (see Chapter 6).

A modern reader always has to keep in mind that the notion of benevolence plays a much less substantial role in Greek ethics, and in Plato in particular, than it does in more recent ways of thinking. In particular, in Plato the desire of a person to organize his society isn't identical with any sort of benevolence. It's certainly not this if by "benevolence" we mean, as we nowadays usually do, a desire that others be happy. The philosopher-rulers' desire to govern the city well is, in the first instance, a desire for it to be well-ordered. That means that each of its parts – analogously to those in an individual's personality – should fulfill its natural function. This desire is a desire for good functional organization.

This isn't to deny that the desire to govern a harmonious city-state is completely disconnected from any aim of people's well-being. The city exists, Plato says, because people aren't self-sufficient, and can't live, let alone live well, in isolation. So in governing the city the rulers are that way enabling their fellow-citizens to attain well-being.

On the other hand, there's not a word in Plato to indicate that when the rulers think about this matter, they should be motivated by any sort of direct satisfaction or gladness about the happiness, in any sense, of any individual people. Even less is the rulers' motivation to govern the city well built up, so to speak, out of their motivation to further the well-being of the individuals whom they encounter directly in their lives. Plato never hints that such a direct person-to-person rapport plays any role at all. To a present-day reader, this fact is bound to call forth a sense of the strangeness of Plato's scheme.

Aristotelian Nature

Criticism of Plato's use of the notion of harmony began early. Aristotle, as I've said, protested against Plato's idea that the better society is always the more unified one. Look once again at *Politics*, II.2:

> Isn't it plain that a city-state may at length have so much unity that it's no longer a city-state? For the nature of a city-state is to be a plurality. (1261a17–19)

He continues a bit later,

> From another viewpoint the extreme unification of the city-state obviously isn't good. For a family is more self-sufficient than an individual, and a city than a family, and a city comes into being only when the community is large enough to be self-sufficient. If, then, self-sufficiency is desirable, less unity is more desirable than more. (1261b10–15)

In fact Plato had himself already accepted one application of this argument. In *Republic* II he'd pointed out that an individual human being isn't self-sufficient. That's why, he'd supposed, the city-state needed to exist.

Aristotle doesn't talk by any means as explicitly about the unity and harmony of an individual as he does about the unity and harmony of a society; this comes in for extensive treatment in his *Politics*. The thesis, "the more harmony the better," doesn't strike him as any more plausible in the former case as in the latter, though he certainly didn't reject the thesis as emphatically as Nietzsche did (see Chapter 2). The danger of conflict, on the personal and on the social level, simply isn't as much of a preoccupation for him as it was for Plato.

To some extent Aristotle replaces the principle "the more harmony, the better" with the kind of benevolent (in the modern sense) motivation that seems to be absent from Plato's political system. The notion of friendship (*philia*) is important in Aristotle's account of how citizens are bound together in society, and how people are attached to each other in smaller groups. Friendship includes a desire for the good of others. On the other hand Aristotle's very far from maintaining the view that the more benevolence, the better, or any principle of universal love. In fact, he even treats the desire for the good of others as like any other desire in requiring to be present only in moderation, not to excess.

Much of the time Aristotle seems to expect a person's life to gain its structure and organization from the fact that he devotes himself to a single activity in which his human nature can be realized. That acts as, so to speak, the filter and organizer that keeps his aims integrated. In the passage of the *Eudemian Ethics* quoted in Chapter 2 he says,

> we must urge everyone who has the power to live according to his own choice to set up for himself an object for the noble life to aim at – honor or reputation or wealth or culture – with reference to which he will perform all his actions. For not to have one's life organized by reference to some end is foolish. (1214b6–11)

Some interpreters contend that Aristotle employs two distinct conceptions of an end, and therefore of happiness, in competition with each other: a "dominant" end and an "inclusive" end. A dominant end is something on which one's life is in some sense focused, though not necessarily so focused that one plans all actions for the sake of pursuing it as much as possible. An inclusive end is an overall plan that includes various different things or activities as constituents. (In a way this is a false contrast, since of course an overall plan can include the selection of one thing as one's main focus.)

According to the traditional and (in my opinion) correct interpretation, Aristotle's view of happiness is one involving the pursuit of a dominant end. The best such end is the realization of theoretical excellence through philosophical thought, or, as second best, of practical excellence, especially as a statesman or publicly active citizen. A person who has the capacity for the theoretical life can best lead it if others – statesmen with practical reason – try, as their dominant end, to organize society so as to allow the theorizer the leisure for contemplative theoretical activity. Aristotle holds (somewhat quixotically) that statesmen will recognize this as a worthy goal of statesmanship, since its goal is to produce the best people and activities possible, and will gladly pursue it.

Plato had believed that in the ideally well-integrated personality, reason grasps philosophically all concepts of value and, in addition, uses them to organize not only its own aims but also its political environment. Aristotle's ideal theorizer, by contrast, isn't independent of the efforts of others. On the contrary, the theorizer relies on the efforts of others to ensure the circumstances in which contemplation is possible. In Aristotle, accordingly, the best way for these two types of people to organize their aims is for each to have a dominant aim.

Aristotle develops and partly revises Plato's idea that a person's reason has two natural functions, practical and theoretical. Aristotle accepts a thesis to the effect that a human being has (as it was later called) a "double nature." As noted (Chapter 2), he holds that human happiness is

> activity of the soul in accordance with excellence, or if there's more than one excellence, in accordance with the best and most complete excellence. (*NE* 1098a17–18)

It does turn out that indeed there's more than one excellence. There's excellence of practical reason, which is exhibited in ethically excellent activity or equivalently (in his view) politics; and there's excellence of theoretical reason too.

To describe the best life, Aristotle thinks he has to determine which of these activities is "better and more complete" than the other. He decides that it's excellence of theoretical reason (*NE* X.7–8). Nevertheless the realization of the other excellence of character, in ethical activity, is good for its own sake too. These two kinds of excellence, however, can't be fully realized together; each activity interferes with the other. Therefore some human good is lost whichever activity one engages in or devotes one's life to. This is, in effect, a denial that all human goods, even the most important, can be fully realized together. Aristotle's best life isn't a life in which goods are coordinated fully, but only partially. For a human life – given the facts about human capacities – there isn't any *ideal* state, only a state that's better than all the others.

It's not even clear, in Aristotle's view, that a fully consistent realization of excellence of character itself is possible. That would depend on, for instance, whether a person could exercise each excellence of character without interfering with the exercise of the other excellences.

In raising this question we're asking, for instance this: Can a person in all cases act fully justly and at the same time fully magnanimously? (The usual later question concerns justice and mercy; but mercy is a Christian virtue, and is not recognized as an excellence by Aristotle.) Or more generally, can the realization of the several excellences of character conflict with each other? If they can, then even "activity in accordance with excellence of character," and hence the kind of happiness that consists in it, can point to different courses of action.

At one point, Aristotle appears to declare roundly that this kind of conflict within practical happiness can't possibly occur:

> It's clear . . . that it's impossible to be good in the strict sense without practical wisdom (*phronêsis*), and impossible to be practically wise without ethical excellence. In this way we can also refute the dialectical argument according to which, someone might contend that the excellences can exist separately from each other. The same man, it might be claimed, isn't best equipped by nature for all the excellences, so that he'll already have acquired one when he hasn't yet acquired another. Now: this is indeed possible in the case of the natural excellences, but not in the case of those in respect of which a man is called good in an unqualified way. For when the one quality, practical wisdom, is present, all the excellences will be too. (*NE* 1144b30–1145a6)

This passage unequivocally rejects a conflict between the possession of one excellence of character and the possession of another.

On the other hand, Aristotle sometimes points to the existence of conflict that arises in the exercise of an excellence of character. Concerning bravery or courage he says:

> death and wounds will be painful to the brave man and against his will, but he will face them because it is noble to do so or because it is base not to do so. And the more he is possessed of virtue in its entirety and the happier he is, the more he will be pained at the thought of death; for life is best worth living for such a man, and he is knowingly losing the greatest of goods, and this is painful. But he is none the less brave . . . (*NE* 1117b7–16)

If this kind of happiness is activity in accordance with excellence of character, it would seem that the greater a person's excellence, the more able he should be to exercise it, and accordingly he should be all the happier. But this passage tells us that the extremely brave person is all the more pained at his own death, because life is so extremely worthwhile for him. This idea doesn't point to a complete harmony of motivation, but a partial one.

Stoic Attitude

The Stoics were every bit as concerned as Plato had been with the consistency of a person's life. However, they adopted a different strategy from Plato's, as did Spinoza much later, partly under their influence. But for all the dissimilarities between Stoic and Platonic doctrines, the Stoics aim primarily at a consistency of aims. One of the Stoic slogans describing the end for a human being is "to live consistently." (Their other main slogan was, "to live consistently with nature," which they held to be equivalent to the former.)

Their way of trying to do this wasn't primarily to filter out or to reduce desires which seemed to disrupt the overall consistency of a person's personality (although that would have been a secondary effect of what they recommended). Instead they took the best condition of a human being to be one in which his reason took a different *attitude* towards these desires, and in particular to their not being satisfied. They thus took another step, beyond the one that Aristotle took, away from talking about how to adjust or control the desires and enjoyments that might disrupt psychic harmony. The Stoic view was that most things that people aim at aren't really good and that the failure to obtain them, and the things that people aim to avoid, aren't really bad. These included the ordinary pleasures and pains of ordinary life. One can put the Stoic point by saying that in their view, these things don't *matter*. They're "indifferent." The Stoics didn't deny that even a person with the right attitude toward life experiences pleasure and pain. But they maintained that such a person, unlike most people, experiences them as things that don't matter, either to his own condition or to the overall condition of the world. In this special sense a person with the right attitude is, in fact, "stoical."

At the opening of his treatise "On the improvement of the understanding," Spinoza espouses much the same position:

> After experience had taught me that everything that normally occurs in social life is vain and futile, and I saw that none of the objects or causes of my fears contained anything good or bad, I resolved to discover whether anything that might be truly good might have the power to communicate itself and which alone could affect the mind . . . and enable me to enjoy continuous, supreme, and eternal happiness.

Spinoza doesn't deny that there are things that a person should enjoy:

> It's the part of a wise man, I say, to refresh himself and restore himself with food and drink, in moderation, and with scents, with beautiful green plants, with decorations, music, sports, the theater, and other such things.

This isn't an ascetic ideal. The point isn't to avoid experiencing or even enjoying such things. Rather, it's to understand what's genuinely valuable and what isn't. Both the Stoics and Spinoza believe that once one can do this, one realizes that the things that normally bother or dismay us aren't important. On the contrary, one realizes that what's important is an understanding of the way in which the universe works – Spinoza emphasizing somewhat more than the Stoics that it's the work of God.

By this strategy of attitude, a result would be accomplished that's in some degree the same as the state that Plato thought was the best for a person to be in. And indeed there are remarks in Plato that are similar to what the Stoics say, for instance this passage (already mentioned) from *Republic* X, about the man whose son has died:

[I]n misfortunes it's best to stay as calm as possible and not become upset by them. First, it isn't clear whether in the end they'll turn out to be good or bad. Second, taking them hard doesn't make the future any better. Third, human affairs aren't worth taking seriously. Finally, grieving hinders what we most need in such circumstances [i.e., deliberation] from occurring as quickly as possible. (604c)

Since in Plato's view the reason can't completely filter out all disruptive feelings and desires, it has to see that those that remain active aren't to be taken seriously. Aside from this, however, Plato places more emphasis than the Stoics do on training and controlling – actually *altering* – one's desires and emotions, and less on adopting a particular attitude towards them.

On the other hand the Stoic strategy has much the same effect as Plato's filter. Desires aren't altered by the Stoic approach, but by treating them and their satisfaction as unimportant, their effect is supposed to be blunted, and the aim of reason to understand the cosmos is allowed to prevail in the attitude of the individual.

The Stoic focus is largely on what one might call "the management of disappointment," whereas Plato had emphasized the tendency of desires to get in each other's way. Plato had stressed the fact that an individual's aims can conflict. He believed that the main problem, therefore, was their *coordination*. In the *Republic* and elsewhere he gives relatively little attention to the problem of their non-satisfaction. He assumed that his scheme for the ideal society would provide the wherewithal for fulfilling basic desires. He didn't worry there about the fact that even a person with well coordinated aims might be unable, because of external circumstances, to fulfill them.

In Stoic thinking, the issue of coping with unfulfilled desires plays a far more prominent role than in Plato or Aristotle. How, they asked, should one react to the unpleasantness of unfulfilled desires, or the other pains and displeasures of life? Their response was, to reiterate, to deny that such things matter. Such things, according to their view, are "indifferent," evaluatively neutral. What matters is virtue and wisdom, they said, consisting in the understanding of one's place in the overall scheme of things, i.e., the *kosmos*. That means: "stoically," i.e., not aiming at things that simply aren't going to happen, and accepting what is going to happen as an inevitable, determined outcome of the way the universe is.

In order to see the significant similarity between the Stoics' and Plato's conceptions of the problem that they face, however, it's important to keep in mind that, like Plato, the Stoics strive explicitly for consistency: a consistent doctrine about the optimal and consistent condition of the person. A Stoic asks that one

> be led on by the marvelous structure of the Stoic system and the miraculous sequence of its topics . . . What can be found in nature – than which nothing is more finished, more nicely ordered – or among things made by handicraft that's more fully integrated than the Stoic system, and fully jointed and welded together? Where do you find a conclusion that doesn't fit with its premises? . . . Where does there fail to be such a close interconnection of one part to another that if you move a single letter, the whole thing falls apart? But indeed not a single thing *could* be moved. (Cicero, *De finibus*, III.74)

The inconsistency to be avoided, according to the Stoic view, would be to think that something that's happened is bad, but at the same time noticing that it has indeed happened and that there's no way in which one can undo it – the past and the present being clearly something that can't be changed. The Stoics held that adopting their stance is the only way in which a self-contradictory attitude, to one's situation and to the world, can be avoided.

Central to the Stoics' exposition of their doctrine was a description of the ideal human condition, which they ascribed to an idealized person whom they called the "Sage" or "Wise Man." This is a person who fully understands the order of the cosmos and realizes that what happens in it is necessitated by its deterministic structure. (The Stoics denied, however, that they thought an individual was not free to decide what to do.) Some Stoics in the second-century AD, notably Panaetius, maintained that each person has a station or role in life, to whose character he must and should conform. This trend of late Stoicism sometimes becomes linked to a kind of fatalistic acceptance. This fits with the Stoic view that the usual "externals" of life aren't good or bad and are of no real value one way or the other.

In spite of the Stoics' ingenuity, in one obvious way their strategy is in danger of being simply an evasion. Perhaps a person who really attained the state of being a wise man would think that his normal physical dissatisfactions don't matter. It's doubtful, though, that any human being can be in this state for long. The proposed attitude towards one's aims and their attainment seems not to comport with how people actually work. Thus one ought to say that people will continue to struggle to get rid of dissatisfactions and conflicts that don't matter. Another such line of thought has been followed by Neoplatonist philosophers and others influenced in similar ways by Plato's philosophy. If one interprets Plato as holding that the sensible world and all in it aren't real, and that the only things that are real are reason and the intelligible Forms that are separate from the physical, one can correspondingly take all conflicts of desires and aims, like the desires and aims and also their objects, to be unreal too. The same outlook is exhibited in the *Bhagavad-Gita* and in Buddhist thinking. In some ways it's similar to the Stoic view that the non-satisfaction of physical desires doesn't matter. It's also subject to an analogous response: to be told that one's pains are unreal is simply incompatible with the way in which they present themselves to the person who has them.

Developments since Antiquity

The aspects of happiness that are treated in this chapter were investigated far more assiduously in antiquity than they have been since, in the West. Aside from the exploration of quantitative hedonism and its offshoots in the nineteenth and twentieth centuries, relatively little of philosophical interest has been developed in the whole period since. This is a surprising fact.

Surprising, and not easily explained. Frequently historians have claimed (falsely, in my opinion; see Chapter 5) that in antiquity, it was universally assumed that everyone pursues only his own happiness as his ultimate goal, and, therefore, that there was no concept of a moral obligation that, even when it required some of his happiness to be sacrificed, a reasonable person might choose to accept. Later, according to this story, that concept did develop, especially in the seventeenth and eighteenth centuries, and so a philosophical examination of it became necessary and did in fact take place (see again Chapter 5).

Even if true, however, this story wouldn't provide a satisfactory account of why ancient treatments of happiness are so much richer than those since. There's no reason why the need to investigate the nature of moral obligation (along with the idea that it can be binding even when it seems to diminish one's own well-being) should induce philosophers to pay less attention to the concept of happiness. Indeed, one might well expect the opposite effect.

The most interesting treatments of happiness between ancient times and Kant seem to me to cluster around two ways of thinking. One, increasingly powerful as time went on, was an attempt to associate the treatment of happiness with the empirical investigation of human psychology. Another, from which that one took over, was a propensity to try to derive the notion of happiness from metaphysical and theological positions. The former line of thought kept the concept pretty close to empirically observable human motivations, sometimes – not surprisingly – at some sacrifice of coherence in the notion. The latter was prone to taking it in the other direction. There was some rough correlation between the former tendency and empiricism (the view that all knowledge is derived from sense perception) in the theory of knowledge, and between the latter tendency and rationalism (the view that some knowledge comes from reason operating independently of sense perception).

Example of this tendency can be found in the writings of the two great philosopher saints, Augustine and Aquinas. This is Augustine's description of *felicitas*:

> The reward of virtue will be God himself, Who gives virtue, and Who has promised Himself to us, than Whom nothing is better or greater. . . . God will be the end of our desires. He will be seen without end, loved without stint, praised without weariness. (*City of God*, XXII.30)

Aquinas' view of the highest or most perfect happiness is expressed as: "perfect human happiness (*beatitudo*) consists in the vision of the divine essence" (*Summa theologica*, IaIIae.5.5).

Aquinas' conception of this kind of happiness is his Christian adaptation of Aristotle's view that the best human happiness is philosophical contemplation. Dante renders Aquinas' conception in the famous lines at the end of *The Divine Comedy*:

> . . . then my mind was struck by light that flashed
> and, with this light, received what it had asked.
>   Here force failed my high fantasy; but my
> desire and will were moved already – like
> a wheel revolving uniformly – by
>   the Love that moves the sun and the other stars.
> (Paradiso, canto 33)

Such conceptions of happiness signify a state that is for a normal human being relatively short-lived. For that reason Aristotle, who held that philosophical thought or contemplation is the best happiness, said that we can engage in it only for short periods, though he did maintained that "we can contemplate truth more continuously than we can *do* anything" (*NE* 1177a23–4). For the same reason just mentioned, a state such as "the vision of the divine essence" isn't presented as, so to speak, the normal sort of happiness even by Aquinas, though it can be promised for the afterlife or ascribed to angels.

Similarly various states of transport or ecstasy aren't usually offered, by either religious or non-religious thinkers, as happiness itself, but rather as the best moments that life has to offer, or are thought of as reserved for the elect, the initiated, or the specially endowed. A life devoted to being in such a state, on the other hand, would count as a kind of happiness in the sense under discussion in this book: a life structured in a certain way, to take various aims into account, with one of them as dominant (in the sense described earlier in the treatment of Aristotle).

The influence of religion can be easily seen in the notion of happiness of a philosopher such as Leibniz, although it's heavily affected by his own elaborate metaphysics. One of the thoughts that plays an especially significant role in Leibniz's thinking is the notion of *perfection*, and a notion of goodness that's closely tied to perfection. He's perhaps most famous for his contention, parodied in Voltaire's *Candide*, that the actual world that God has created is the best of all possible worlds. Accordingly it's unsurprising to find him employing perfection in his account of human well-being.

And employ it he does, to the point of shaping his whole view of pleasure and happiness around it. Leibniz rejected the idea that it's better to be unmoved by one's own pleasure or delight but moved rather by God's will alone. In this view he thought he saw a false contrast:

> We must realize that this conflicts with the nature of things. For the impulse to action arises from a striving for perfection, the perception of which is pleasure, and no action or will has any other basis. (Leibniz 1969: 424)

Two contentions appear here. One is that our aim in action is always perfection. The other is that what we feel as pleasure is a sense of perfection of something. The striking thing about this view is that it finds in the experience of pleasure a content or meaning – a sense of perfection – that doesn't present itself to a person without reflection, but is supplied by the rather particular metaphysical framework that Leibniz espouses.

A related line of thought shows itself in Spinoza. He defines "joy" (*laetitia*) as "the passion by which the mind passes to a greater perfection." And he asserts, "Joy is a human being's passage from a lesser to a greater perfection. Sadness is a human being's from a greater to a lesser perfection" (*Ethics* 3da2–3).

Perfection enters into the account of joy in two different ways. It's the result or manifestation of an increase in the perfection of the person who experiences the joy; and it's also part of the content of the experience of joy.

However, one might well object that pleasure or joy simply and obviously *isn't* a sense of the perfection of anything. If that's right then both Leibniz and Spinoza misdescribe the phenomenology of pleasure and allied experiences. Their views about our capacity accurately to describe our perceptions, however, allow them to ignore our experiences to some fair extent. Both of them – especially Spinoza in his parallelism concerning mind and body – held in general that our experiences can be associated with states of the world (including our bodies) that aren't immediately apparent to us. Leibniz, for one, has a powerful way of trying to support such an idea: the notion of a "confused perception." All sorts of conscious states, he holds, can be said to be confused perceptions of non-conscious states of affairs that would seem, in fact, to be utterly unconnected with the conscious states, and assuredly not to be part of their content. So neither Spinoza nor Leibniz would necessarily regard our interpretation or description of our experience as trustworthy.

Views about happiness such as those of Augustine, Aquinas, Leibniz, and Spinoza – along with many others – fit a moral position established by religion together with a metaphysical theory of the universe. Built into these theories are respective ways of selecting, from among the aims, enjoyments, and values that human beings actually have or accept, those that square with or are recommended by those theories.

Such accounts of happiness or enjoyment therefore have no need to incorporate a story, an additional "filter" or any other such device, in order to tell us which aims to satisfy or which enjoyments to prize. That work is done by the metaphysical view that's thought to imply or yield that account of happiness. So, for example, Leibniz builds into his metaphysical theory the perfection of God and the world that he created. There's no need for him – as there was for Plato – to examine the phenomenon of pleasure in order to determine which pleasures are allowable in a harmonious or right-thinking or right-acting personality. From Leibniz's standpoint, it was already a given – by the point in his exposition at which he was explaining what pleasure is – that such a person would accept his version of Christianity and his own metaphysics along with it. Both Leibniz and his readers were going to assume, as a matter of course, that the best condition of a human being would be one that would fit with Christian doctrine, even though there would be disagreements about how to construe it.

In contrast to the foregoing, a different tendency shows itself in Locke (in a late manuscript note). It's one thing to regard an experience as pleasant, Locke holds firmly, and quite another to regard it as morally righteous:

> That which has very much confounded men about the will and its determination has been the confounding of the notion of moral rectitude and giving it the name of moral good. The pleasure that a man takes in any action or expects as a consequence of it is indeed a good in the self able and proper to move the will. But the moral rectitude of it considered barely in itself is not good or evil nor any way moves the will, but as pleasure or pain either accompanies the action itself or is looked on to be a consequence of it. Which is evident from the punishments and rewards which God has annexed to moral rectitude or pravity as proper motives to the will, which would be needless if moral rectitude were in itself good and moral pravity evil.

Locke makes a notable effort here to take pleasure and pain not to be laden, so to speak, with moral content. Enjoying is one thing, morally approving is another. Moreover saying that someone's enjoying something isn't to say that what he's enjoying is morally praiseworthy. Locke's saying, or moving in the direction of saying, that pleasure is simply an empirical phenomenon (Chapter 6).

You might expect that the philosophers who took this view of pleasure would be empiricists, and that those who explained it in terms of a metaphysical or theological theory incorporating evaluative notions would be rationalists. That's not always so. Spinoza and Leibniz were rationalists, certainly. Descartes was too, yet he comes closer to Locke on this matter than he does to the other two.

Descartes distinguishes sharply between the supreme good, which is a condition of a person's will, and the feeling of contentment that arises as a result of one's having attained this condition:

> [T]here is a difference between happiness, the supreme good, and the final end or goal toward which our actions ought to tend. For happiness is not the supreme good, but presupposes it, being the contentment or satisfaction of the mind which results from possessing it. (1991: 261)

As Descartes remarked, this seems like a combination of Stoic and Epicurean views (1991: 325). But in any case, unlike Leibniz and Spinoza, Descartes doesn't identify pleasure with something that must be described by means of concepts supplied by his own doctrines.

Descartes's thinking on this matter, by the way, illustrates the point made earlier about the greater richness of ancient ideas about happiness. The views about happiness that form part of these early modern philosophers' doctrines make very substantial use of elements from ancient philosophy: Plato, Aristotle, Stoicism, and Epicureanism. This is no bad thing. All good philosophers have always used plenty of material that lay ready to hand. One can't help thinking, on reading what these philosophers say about happiness, that when writing on this particular subject they took over only those ideas from Greek antiquity that served their purposes – purposes that, if of Christian intent, would have no derivation in Greek philosophy. They exercised their originality mainly on other topics instead – natural law and obligation being just two examples – and also on what are nowadays called the "interfaces" between those topics and the ancient ideas about happiness that they exploited.

Just as Descartes illustrates the proposition that a rationalist in epistemology may employ a concept of pleasure that doesn't incorporate an a priori metaphysics, Herbert Spencer shows that a supposedly empiricist thinker can hold a view of pleasure while ignoring empirical evidence against it. Spencer claimed to derive his ethical views from empirical knowledge, that is, from a doctrine about evolution. Nonetheless he accepts the equivalence of "pleasant" and "conducive to self-preservation" *not* on the basis of anything like direct observation of what happens when something seems pleasant to someone. Rather, Spencer accepts the equivalence on the say-so of a theory (his own particular interpretation – a misguided one – of Darwin's theory of evolution). He accordingly bypasses any direct observational investigation into whether people actually do regard as pleasant things that actually *are* conducive to their self-preservation. If he had trusted observation he would have found considerable evidence against the generalization, which is only broadly true, that people find pleasant whatever contributes to their self-preservation.

In general one can say that, during the early modern period of philosophy, empirical and metaphysical-theological considerations were intricately mixed in many people's thinking about happiness and pleasure. Empirical and metaphysical-theological ideas were mixed together in practically all areas of thought during this period, as people were trying to gain clarity on what role, if any, religious views ought to play in the investigation of the natural world.

A good example of this increasing attention to the observation of people, though without an explicit demarcation of where it's applicable, can be found in Butler, in the early eighteenth century. He contends that as a matter of observable fact, human beings do desire the happiness of others. He doesn't postulate this as a requirement of reason, or of God's design for the world (though he certainly thought that it was the latter). He treats it as a plain fact which we can observe, just as one can observe that people desire to eat or drink.

Like Locke, Shaftesbury, and others since the time of Plato, Butler recognized and stressed, as a natural fact about human beings, that they have a plurality of aims and desires. Though it's been fashionable since this period to employ the notion of "interest" or "self-interest" to try to explain a wide range of human behavior, all three of these figures insisted that there's no single monolithic motive designated by such a term, or even, for that matter, by the word "pleasure." Only a verbal trick, Shaftesbury thinks, induces anyone to say that pleasure motivates all actions:

> when will and pleasure are synonymous; when everything which pleases us is called pleasure, and we never choose or prefer but as we please; 'tis trifling to say, 'Pleasure is our good'. For this has as little meaning as to say, 'We choose what we think eligible'; and 'We are pleased with what delights or pleases us'. (*Characteristics of Men . . .* , II, p. 29)

In fact a person's happiness is made up of the fulfillment of multifarious motives (Shaftesbury, *Inquiry . . .* , pp. 255–6; Butler, Sermon XI). Among the desires of any normal person is "benevolence," the desire for the happiness of others. This, Shaftesbury thinks, is shown to us by ordinary observation. The satisfaction of this desire can accordingly be seen to be a component of a person's happiness, just as much as the satisfaction of one's desire for food or for fame is.

Like Plato, Butler stresses the importance of the question of how a person's various desires are coordinated with each other. Some appetites (Butler follows Plato in saying) can disrupt a person's life.

Moreover Butler recognizes that, as a matter of fact, the mere presence in someone of a desire for others' happiness doesn't guarantee that that desire will be stronger than his other desires, or will exercise a determinative influence on action. Therefore the presence of that desire in someone doesn't guarantee that he'll be, overtly, especially benevolent.

Butler maintains, however, that "conscience" is capable of coordinating all other desires including benevolence, much as Plato said that reason does. Given the facts about the natural strengths of the various human motivations, Butler supposes that in favorable circumstances people will have well-coordinated desires, and will also (through the combined action of conscience and benevolence) cooperate with each other. (This belief of Butler's distinguishes him from Locke, who appears to posit no coordinating agency within the personality.)

I emphasize the comparison just alluded to between Plato and Butler. According to Plato the harmonizing factor in the personality is reason, whereas according to Butler it's conscience. What's the difference? In both, the coordinating factor considers the well-being of others (either through benevolence in Butler, or the wish to organize the city in Plato). Moreover in both the coordinating factor organizes one's own motivations so that they don't interfere with each other. Is there, then, any significant difference between them? Or does Butler's view have the structure simply of a Christianized Platonism? That's not an easy question to answer, because of the unsettled boundary in Butler between the facts about people that we can discover by observation and those that we have to determine by our own reasoning.

In Hume, one finds greater reliance on empirical observation for information about people's motivations and aims, and likewise in Adam Smith. In them a different sort of psychological factor seems to take over some of the burden from what Butler calls "conscience." What allows people to get along with each other, they believe, isn't reason, but instead primarily the desire to be pleasing to others, or a sense of belonging to society, or the desire for other people's "approval" (to use their word). The latter idea, which is especially prominent in Smith, goes back to the Stoic thesis that a person seeks to be consistent with nature as a whole, and the further claim that part of that consistency is a matter of fitting into society and into humankind.

The Kantian Critique of the Concept of Happiness

Kant has a far more distinct idea of which concepts are applied by empirical observation and which aren't, and is far more actively concerned with getting clear on the question. For him, happiness is an empirical concept. But that fact lends to the concept a lack of clarity that, Kant believes, puts it in a certain way outside the purview of rigorous reasoning.

In the *Grounding for the Metaphysics of Morals*, Kant contends that the concept of happiness isn't graspable by reason. He says:

> [M]en cannot form any definite and certain concept of the sum of satisfaction of all inclinations that is called happiness. (399)

and

> unfortunately the concept of happiness is such an indeterminate one that though everyone wishes to attain happiness, yet he can never say definitely and consistently what it is that he really wishes and wills. (418)

As a result the concept isn't of much use for the fully rational evaluation or planning of one's life. Though he seems to qualify or back off from this position in the *Critique of Practical Reason*, this attitude toward the notion had a significant effect on the subsequent treatment of it.

Just after the last passage quoted, Kant says,

> The reason for this is that all the elements belonging to the concept of happiness are unexceptionally empirical . . . while for the idea of happiness there is required an absolute whole, a maximum of well-being in my present and in every future condition.

The reason that Kant gives for our inability to conceive of this absolute whole is this:

> Now it is impossible for the most insightful and at the same time most powerful, but nonetheless finite, being to frame here a determinate concept of what it is that he really wills. Does he want riches? How much anxiety, envy, intrigue might he not thereby bring down on his head? . . . Or long life? Who guarantees that it would not be a long misery? Or health at least? How often has infirmity of the body kept one from excesses into which perfect health would have allowed him to fall, and so on? In brief, he is not able on any principle to determine with complete certainty what will make him truly happy, because to do so would require omniscience. (*Critique of Practical Reason*, Bk I, ch. i, §8, Remark 2)

The difficulty is that applying the idea of happiness requires certain prediction of the consequences of this or that action or state. But certainty isn't obtainable, Kant contends, in empirical predictions. The line of thought is continued in the *Critique of Practical Reason*:

> The principle of happiness can indeed give maxims, but never maxims which are competent to be laws of the will, even if universal happiness were made the object. For, since knowledge of this rests on mere data of experience, as each judgment of it depends on the very changeable opinion of each person, it can give general but never universal rules . . . (Ibid.)

In spite of this, Kant nevertheless holds that happiness is the appropriate reward for virtue. Happiness isn't of itself good. For "it always presupposes conduct in accordance with the moral law as its condition." Nevertheless,

> ... virtue and happiness together constitute the possession of the highest good for one person, and happiness in exact proportion to morality (as the worth of a person and his worthiness to be happy) constitutes the highest good of a possible world. (*Critique of Practical Reason*, Bk. II, ch. ii)

so although happiness isn't of itself good or the highest good, it's a component of the state of affairs that's the highest good.

Dynamic Conceptions

In discussing Greek ethics, I said that all of its conceptions of happiness are in a sense static. Although it's assumed that happiness involves undergoing changes and engaging dynamically in activities, nevertheless the condition of happiness is taken to be one that can be fully described at one time, and indeed in advance of a person's leading his life. The happy life can then be thought of as the carrying out of that plan, or the subsequent fulfilling of that description.

A number of steps away from this kind of conception of happiness have taken place in more recent times, that is, in the nineteenth century or later. Its historical beginnings aren't evident. Hegel's a possible originator of a dynamic concept of happiness that changes over an individual's life. On the other hand, what Hegel says about happiness – while it might fit with his belief in the unfolding of the spirit over the course of history – doesn't suggest anything about the development of the individual. Hegel says, in his *Encyclopedia* of 1817,

> Happiness is the confused representation of the satisfaction of all drives, which, however, are either entirely or partially sacrificed and [preferred to each other]. Their mutual limitation, on the one hand, is a mixture of qualitative and quantitative determination; on the

other hand, since the inclination is a subjective and immediate basis for determination, it is . . . subjective feeling and good pleasure which must [be decisive]. . . . (§396)

This sounds more like Kant's view, that happiness isn't a well-defined concept, than like an approach to a dynamic conception.

Sidgwick comes early in the line of philosophers who stress that the changes in a person's life play a crucial role in his thinking about his own happiness. Sidgwick urged the importance of the fact that

as long as Time is a necessary form of human existence, it can hardly be surprising that human good should be subject to the condition of being realized in successive parts. (*The Methods of Ethics*, p. 407n.)

This point he presses against the thesis, advocated by T. H. Green, that the chief good must be something which "can be conceived in possession," i.e., possessed all at once. Green used his thesis to argue against hedonism, since as he points out, pleasure is experienced in episodes distributed over different times. However, the scope of the disagreement is broader. Sidgwick's claim is that happiness, whether it is pleasure or something else, needn't be something that can be possessed all at once. Not all philosophers who've investigated happiness have accepted this thesis about it, but it seems to me plain that most of them have. (Contrary to Green, it's not in conflict with Aristotle's view that happiness is an "activity" or "actuality.")

To assert that happiness is realized over time isn't in and of itself a departure from the static conception of happiness. But the assertion can easily lead to such a departure. What's required is the thought that planning for a temporal stretch of happiness (or unhappiness) has to be carried out over time and under changing conditions. Once one realizes that, one sees that it's impossible to have before one's mind a full plan of life that can remain unchanged for the whole period through which one lives, and that only needs to be carried out. Rather, whatever plan one has must contain, somehow, a way of providing for its own revision.

Sidgwick is a (loosely quantitative) hedonist. (He's torn, in fact, between hedonist egoism and hedonist utilitarianism.) Accordingly he has a theoretically fixed and unchangeable plan to carry out the maximization of pleasure. However he does make one point that causes the plan to be less than completely rigid. He recognizes that

> a rational method of attaining the end at which it aims requires that we should to some extent put it out of sight and not directly aim at it. (*The Methods of Ethics*, p. 136; see also Chapter 3)

This implies that a person might need unavoidably to adopt a shifting perspective on deliberation. At times one would need to think explicitly about how to increase one's pleasure; but at other times one would need to avoid thinking about it. The latter episodes would presumably need, sometimes, to be set up by prior planning not to think about gaining pleasure. Some philosophers have contended that to adopt this kind of shifting perspective is incoherent. What it seems to me to show, rather, is just that given the facts about human beings, the perspective of deliberation about one's happiness can't be static.

It's easy to see in the thinking of the twentieth century a move away from the notion of static perspective for deliberation and evaluation, toward ever more dynamic conceptions. It's even become a cliché to remark on this fact. Jean-Paul Sartre's aphorism, "Existence precedes essence," and the Existentialist thinking that accompanies it, express this kind of thinking, as do many other rejections of fixed points in ethics. So do some of the reflections of Husserl and others, including Sartre, who have worked in his wake.

We start, as before, with the fact of the plurality of and conflicts among a person's aims, etc., as they present themselves. We start also with the sense that satisfactions, etc., need somehow to be pulled together to enable an inclusive evaluation of a person's condition. In addition, as I've said, questions arise as to the point of view from which this pulling together and evaluating is to be done. The issue now under examination concerns the time of the evaluation, given that life is temporally extended.

It's common to remark on the fact that the concept of happiness allows for assessments of one's condition from various temporal vantage points. We can evaluate someone's overall condition either at a particular time, or over a stretch of his or her life, or over that life as a whole. Think of the difference between Solon and the women in the coffee house (Chapter 1). Nevertheless further facts about these evaluations still have to be taken into account.

The range of perspectives for assessing a life, especially one's own life, is greater than is suggested by the simple dichotomy of present moment and whole life. Our assessments don't just divide up into those that say how someone's doing right now and those that survey his or her life as a whole.

Our actual way of thinking about these things is much more complicated. For instance, while a person is alive, an assessment of a whole life, just like an assessment of a particular present stage of it, is made from a time *within* the period of the ongoing life itself. Solon pressed people to judge whether a person was happy from outside that life, after its end. But people also try to evaluate their whole lives (and those of others), to the extent that they can, from within them too. So, at the least, we have a trichotomy: assessing how things are going now, assessing now how one's life seems to stack up as a whole, and assessing a life as a whole from a point outside it. From the standpoint of deliberation about what to do, the important standpoints are the first two.

Recall the point made earlier about the influence on Plato's and Aristotle's views of the fact that they both directed schools. The clients of these schools were wealthy gentlemen seeking an education for their sons that would launch their careers. Accordingly both Plato and Aristotle sometimes pictured the decision about what type of life to live as involving the presentation to a gentleman of a plan for the life of his son. The plan for life would be made, the course would be set, and the ongoing activity would be pictured as carrying out a plan that had already been made.

The important observation that our plans are in a sense incomplete is articulated clearly in the late twentieth century, in a way reminiscent of Sartre's and other existentialist ideas, by Michael Bratman:

> We do not, of course, promote coordination [of aims] and extend the influence of deliberation by means of plans that specify, once and for all, everything we are to do in the future. Such total plans are obviously beyond our limits. Rather, we typically settle on plans that are *partial* and then fill them in as need be and as time goes by. This characteristic *incompleteness* of our plans . . . creates the need for a kind of reasoning characteristic of planning agents: reasoning that takes initial partial plans as given and aims at filling them in with appropriate specification of means, preliminary steps, or just relatively more specific courses of action. (1987: 3)

It's struck many readers that the conditions of life today, especially in the United States but also in many other countries, don't fit the presuppositions of stability that traditional pictures of happiness rest on. Plans for careers and lives are still made. However, in many societies they're expected to be less stable than they were in earlier times. Flexibility is called for. Decisions are made and carried out partially, then revised, sometimes in directions that couldn't have been foreseen when the decision was made.

But of course the world has never been stable enough for a life to be planned out in advance down to the very last detail. Even in antiquity human beings' plans and intentions were always to some extent open, even if philosophers' descriptions of them haven't always made that clear.

Similarly someone's conception of what it is or would be to carry out one and the same particular action or project successfully will often change over time. It will change between the time when the project is initially conceived, and the time when it's completed, and subsequent times when it's remembered. Not only is life, as Sidgwick said, "realized in successive parts," the evaluation of one's life is too (even if it can be reconstructed *ex post* as a pattern of prospective changes foreseen at a single time). Moreover, one's conception of the standards by which the evaluation is made typically changes also.

This fact throws into some confusion the frequently drawn contrast between assessments of one's condition at one time and the assessment of a whole life. A whole life can be assessed from many different points from within it. Solon assumed, as far as one can tell, that if the whole life was to be evaluated, that had to be done at the end of it, and Aristotle assumed the same thing. But it isn't at all clear that that's right, even given the obvious fact that more of the facts are open to being surveyed later than earlier.

One philosopher who explored this matter in a detailed way was C. I. Lewis, the early-twentieth-century pragmatist, some of whose reflections go back to earlier pragmatists like Peirce and Dewey. In the present chapter I've already quoted an observation of his that illustrates a seeming difficulty in quantitative hedonism's failure to attend to the structures within which pleasures occur:

> One could not . . . by selecting from amongst Beethoven's symphonies the three movements which are rated highest, and juxtaposing these, create a better symphony than Beethoven ever wrote. Musically juxtaposed passages qualify one another. (1946: 496)

That remark is pertinent to the present issue. The value of a set of episodes in a life – thought of as their contribution to overall happiness – can't be equated to the value of a series that one would get if one simply went through those episodes one after another. Nor is the contribution of a single episode as it actually occurs in its chronological context the contribution that it would make, if any, to such series. Our plans, however, usually can't fully determine even so much as the chronological order of occurrence of the episodes that are essential to them.

Lewis emphasized also that when a person evaluates his condition, he generally doesn't think only about how he's doing right at the moment, nor simply about his life as a whole. He makes, rather, an assessment that combines both in a complicated way:

> a life good on the whole, which is our continuing and rational concern, is something whose goodness or badness is at no moment immediately disclosed, but can be contemplated only by some imaginative or synthetic engagement of its on-the-whole quality. (1946: 483)

This idea goes beyond Sidgwick's point, that "human good [is] subject to the condition of being realized in successive parts." As Lewis puts one of the further implications,

> A fortiori this is beyond simply setting a structure for life and then asking, overall and from outside it, whether a life will conform to it or has done so. (p. 483)

If we follow Plato in thinking that our array of aims needs to have a structure, it turns out that the requisite structure is much more complex than it might have seemed. Despite the pressure that we always feel to form an integrated assessment of a human being's condition, it's not evident that we have a way of forming an integrated view of a structure like this one (see Chapter 7). This is still something for philosophers and others to think about.

Chapter 5

Morality, Happiness, and Conflict

Happiness and Morality

The most discussed objection to the idea of an all-inclusive assessment of a person's condition is the notion of *morality*. Many philosophers have maintained – Kant most famously, though he's far from being the only one or the first – that if we're thinking about ways in which a person's condition can be assessed, we shouldn't focus on happiness. One such contention is Kant's view that happiness is in a sense not a coherent concept, and that rational evaluations have to do with moral features: of a person's will or of his actions instead. Another is that there are two assessments to be made, one of a person's happiness and the other of his or her moral status. It's part of this latter idea that there's no way of pooling the two evaluations to get a single one of the person's condition.

If we think of how happy a person is as initially laying claim to be the overall "score" of his state, then these two contentions hold, respectively, that the only reasonable score is that of moral status (happiness not being even a coherent scoring-system), and that there are two rival scoring systems, one of morality and the other of happiness, with no way of combining the two scores or adding them together to get a single, overall one. This talk of "scoring" is a picturesque way of describing ways of organizing considerations pertinent to evaluation.

What works most strongly against the idea of a single, inclusive assessment of one's moral condition, in most minds, is the potential conflict between an assessment according to its standards and assessments of other kinds that normally fall under the label "happiness." The distinction between moral and other evaluations may be felt to be neither completely clear nor entirely sharp nor easy to explain or even to justify. Nevertheless there are clear enough cases of the distinction to make the potential for conflict obvious.

As noted earlier (Chapter 1), other types of evaluation, too, pose threats to the inclusiveness of the assessment that's linked to the concept of happiness. For instance various notions falling under the label "perfection" seem to do so. Beauty is one such; so is athletic prowess; and there are many others. So is the kind of character that Nietzsche was interested in, however it should be labeled.

These threats to the all-inclusiveness of happiness as a dimension of assessment, however, have never seemed so serious as the one from morality. In spite of Nietzsche's sometimes disdainful attitude toward making happiness one's aim, for instance, even his conception of a certain kind of greatness or grandeur, is possible to understand as itself a kind of happiness – just a different kind of happiness from the one that most people are after. Given the obvious fact that happiness in the normal sense can be thought to embrace various components, it's not at all hard to think that a Nietzschean condition can be one of them, or even the pre-eminent one.

The contrast between assessments of happiness and moral character, however, can't so readily be eliminated as the one between happiness and the Nietzschean conception. Philosophers such as Kant have tried, moreover, to erect systematic barriers to block any such bridges, though it's controversial to what extent they've succeeded.

This contrast is usually expressed by means of two families of expressions: moral obligation versus one's own good or happiness, or duty versus interest, or what one ought to do or be versus what one would do or be if only one's own benefit were at stake, or between one's obligations and what one wants to do or have, or between duty and inclination, and so on. These distinctions certainly don't always line up with each other, but they're obviously closely related to each other. Pre-reflectively everyone understands the intended contrast or contrasts – better, indeed, than one usually understands the philosophically central but problematic terminology.

Nowadays many readers are prone to link the contrast with the name of Kant, and his distinction, or distinctions, between duty and inclination or duty and happiness. But the contrast is older than Kant, and it's a bad idea to associate it too closely with him, since he attaches certain particular features to it that derive from his own special positions on other topics. Better to think of the contrast, or contrasts, in a broader way. At any rate, it's observable earlier in, just for example, the writings of Samuel Clarke and Joseph Butler, and, although under different terminology, in Aquinas and in much Greek thought. The overall situation in Christianity is well summed up by Sidgwick:

> generally, in the ages of Christian faith, it has been obvious and natural to hold that the realization of virtue is essentially an enlightened and far-seeing pursuit of happiness for the agent. . . . [However,] this is only one side or element of the Christian view: the opposite doctrine, that an action done from motives of self-interest is not properly virtuous, has continually asserted itself as either openly conflicting or in some manner reconciled with the former. (*The Methods of Ethics*, p. 120)

Even if you don't believe in a metaphysical notion of "human nature," it's easy to think that the contrast is widespread enough among people that it has to figure in any discussion of them that's not restricted in some special way.

It seems to me that Sidgwick's description applies not just to Christianity, but to the thinking of people in general. People waver, I think, between two outlooks. One is the sense that moral considerations are external to happiness, so that there can be a conflict between (for example) what it's morally right to do and what's conducive to one's happiness. The other is the sense that there's no conflict here, either because happiness, being all-inclusive, therefore includes being moral or morally upright, or because being morally upright guarantees being happy (perhaps through divine agency), or for both of these reasons together. Most people seem to be able somehow to adopt both of these two outlooks side by side, perhaps because one can avoid thinking about their lack of fit with each other. This is not, I think, the area in which people's thoughts are at their most hard-edged.

The most difficult thing to grasp about the idea of morality as its own special kind of aim or consideration, lying outside of an interest in one's own happiness, has always been to explain how such moral considerations can be "binding." How, many ask, can it make sense or be reasonable – not be simply crazy – to do what you morally ought to do, even if you don't want to do it and think that it works against your happiness?

It's taken a long time for well-developed answers to this question to emerge. Some efforts were made by Plato, and somewhat weaker ones by Aristotle. Plenty of philosophers – Shaftesbury and Butler are good examples – were aware of the conceptual distinction between doing what you morally ought to do and seeking your own happiness. A real breakthrough, though, came in Kant's work. Kant's crucial move was his effort to show how the idea of moral obligation can be held to be generated out of a notion of universality, which was (he thought) a part of reason itself. Kant accompanied this with a proposal as to why the motivations that normally induce people not to conform to morality, such as desires or what he called 'inclinations', should be regarded as unpersuasive.

Before Kant there was virtually always a realization that someone's moral obligations and his or her happiness are conceptually distinct considerations, and can even conflict. No one, however, had much of a philosophical explanation to give of *why* obligation provides a good reason to do something that works against one's happiness. The absence of such an explanation contributed to making some thinkers shaky about the existence of the distinction itself.

The Conflict in Antiquity

According to one widespread view, the ancient Greeks had no conception of morality as a consideration distinct from, and potentially conflicting with, one's own happiness. Rather, this story says, the Greeks all thought that one's happiness is the only rational basis for deliberation. As Sidgwick puts it,

> in the whole ethical controversy of ancient Greece . . . it was assumed on all sides that a rational individual would make the pursuit of his own good his supreme aim. (*Outlines of the History of Ethics*, p. 198)

This idea is often put by saying that Greek ethics is *eudaimonist*. In the terms employed here, this is equivalent to saying that in Greek ethics, one's own happiness is indeed assumed by rational people to be the single and all-inclusive evaluation of a person's condition. In my opinion this description of the Greeks is mistaken. It seems to me that although some Greeks, including some Greek philosophers, held the view that Sidgwick alludes to, the distinction and potential conflict between obligation and happiness was widely recognized, though it wasn't well accounted for.

The Stoics, I think, did fit Sidgwick's description fairly well, though what they say shows that others didn't. The Stoics maintain that the only good for a person is virtue, including justice. They also held that the end of a human being is "consistency with nature" or "consistency" (Chapter 4), and they included within this "consistency" being virtuous and adhering to moral and social standards. They even try to show that one can't really even *conceive* of a difference between virtue and benefit to oneself. Through all of this, however, they plead their case in a way that shows, I think, that much of their audience was assumed to believe that these things clearly are different, and can clash with each other. For they acknowledge that the identification of good and virtue is a "paradox."

The widespread impression that Greek ethics is eudaimonist is due, I think, to a misinterpretation of it encouraged largely by Kant and Hegel. Kant rarely refers to Greek ethics and seems to have paid little serious attention to it. He believed that one's happiness is entirely the wrong reason for abiding by one's moral obligations. Rather, he thought, one should do what one's morally obligated to do "out of respect for the moral law." Since the Greeks certainly didn't have *this* idea – either of the moral law in Kant's sense or of 'respect' for it – Kant could easily conclude that they didn't really have the notion of moral obligation at all. And they *didn't* have *his* notion of it.

Greek ethics is also full of attempts to show how abiding by moral standards *is* normally and indeed almost always conducive to one's happiness. This is true, for instance, of Plato's *Republic* and Aristotle's *Nicomachean Ethics*. That doesn't show, however, that Plato and Aristotle didn't acknowledge that moral considerations can sometimes conflict with one's own well-being.

To Kant, however, the fact that these philosophers were so ready to argue for moral uprightness on the basis of one's happiness was a further indication that they didn't understand the notion of moral obligation, or the sharp difference between it and morality. So it was easy for him to assume that their view was eudaimonist through and through.

Hegel and his followers – a British example is T. H. Green – had a quite different reason for interpreting Greek ethics in this way. Hegel believed that Kant was quite wrong to see a potential conflict between moral obligation and the satisfaction of one's own desires or "inclinations." Hegel thought that he could appeal to the Greeks to oppose Kant in this arena. He thought that if you truly grasped the concept of morality, quite otherwise than as Kant had, and if you also grasped the concept of your own benefit, you'd see that the latter *includes* or *contains* the former, and that therefore an attempt to gain your own happiness would have to include an attempt to conform to morality (in the correctly understood sense).

This is precisely the kind of eudaimonist view that Hegel and subsequent Hegelians have normally attributed to Greek philosophers.

Hegel thus agreed with Kant verbally, that the Greeks accepted eudaimonism, but he took a different view of what their eudaimonism amounted to. Ever since, it's been common to describe Greek ethics as eudaimonist in one sense or another.

Eudaimonist interpretations of Greek thought, however, run up against contrary evidence. It takes the form of passages in which Greek philosophers, as well as non-philosophical writers, show an awareness that considerations of morality and of one's happiness are distinct and can oppose each other. There are examples of this awareness in Plato and Aristotle.

Plato says the following things about the philosopher-rulers in his ideal city. First, he says,

> We should examine then, with this in mind, whether our aim in establishing our guardians should be to give them the greatest happiness, or whether we should in this matter look to *the whole city* and see how *its greatest happiness* can be secured. We must compel and persuade the auxiliaries and the guardians to be excellent performers of their own task, and so with all the others. As the whole city grows and is well governed, we must leave it to nature to provide each group with its share of happiness. (*Republic* 420b–c, my emphasis)

Then later on he says,

> For the fact is . . . if you can discover a way of life that's *better than* governing for the prospective governors, a well arranged city becomes a possibility. . . . (520e–521a, my emphasis)

The upshot is this. The rulers' task is to govern the city. To perform it, they need to understand justice and the good (533–4, 540–1). To do that, Plato thinks, it must also be part of their function to philosophize extensively. But they have to philosophize before they begin to govern, so the two activities have to be separable temporally. Moreover Plato thinks that the two activities interfere with each other (governing gets in the way of thinking about philosophy). Therefore they can't be pursued well at the same time.

But by philosophizing the rulers discover two things. The first is that philosophizing is the most pleasant activity – far more so than governing – and would make them happier. The second is that in spite of that they're obligated to rule. So ruling requires them to philosophize, and philosophy makes clear to them both that they're obliged to rule, and also that philosophizing is better for them to engage in than ruling. There's the conflict.

Aristotle, too, paints a picture that's analogous in the crucial respect. The best sort of happiness for a human being, he says, is philosophical thinking or "contemplation" (*theoria*):

> Happiness extends . . . just as far as contemplation, and happiness belongs to people in proportion as contemplation does, not accidentally but by virtue of the contemplation, since this is itself estimable. So happiness would be some form of contemplation. (*NE* 1178b28–31)

"But in a secondary way the life in accordance with [practical excellence] is happy" (1178a8–9): a secondary sort of happiness is constituted by political activity.

Political activity is other-regarding, and conforms with the ethical standards that Aristotle presupposes. Contemplation, on the other hand, is largely self-confined (though Aristotle sometimes presents it as being done in the company of a few friends or colleagues). Both kinds of activity are realizations of human excellence, i.e., of the capacity to reason, practically in one case and theoretically in the other (see Chapters 1 and 2). So both are forms of happiness. However, political activity distracts one from philosophical thinking. A person can't engage in both of them fully (just as Plato had contended too). So to that degree they conflict. In this situation Aristotle recommends the more self-regarding life devoted to contemplation over the other-regarding political life.

Although Aristotle says that the happiest life is the life devoted to philosophical thought, he also indicates that since a person can't think all the time, such a life will also contain scope for other-regarding excellences of character. It will contain, in other words, two main aims, though contemplation will be the dominant aim.

In both Plato and Aristotle, then, we have a recognition of a conflict between two values: the public, ethical, and other-regarding activity of politics and the more self-regarding activity of philosophical thought. Plato maintains that from their philosophical thinking itself, philosopher-rulers can learn that they're obliged to engage in politics, because they're fortunate enough to live in a good society. (No such obligation falls on philosophers who don't live in such a society, Plato maintains, and they're best advised to stay clear of politics.) Aristotle, on the other hand, doesn't think that philosophical thought provides any such demonstration of the need to live a life devoted to politics. On the contrary, it's simply the best activity, and engaging in it leads one away from political activity.

In the face of this conflict, it turns out that Plato and Aristotle come out on different sides. Plato's on the side of political activity under special circumstances (i.e., in the ideal city-state), and Aristotle is for philosophical thought. In Plato, however, politics is obligatory and just for the philosopher-rulers, even though it doesn't make them as happy as they'd be philosophizing. Here we find something analogous to the modern conflict between duty and happiness. We also see something not dissimilar to the idea that when the conflict actually breaks out, then, as many moderns have maintained, duty should take precedence over one's own happiness.

Later Obstacles to the Articulation and Explanation of the Conflict

In spite of the awareness in Greek ethics of possible clashes between these two distinct considerations – ethical standards and an individual's happiness – and in spite of the sense of tension that Sidgwick describes and that we see in Aquinas and other Christian writers, a long time was needed for a picture of two independent kinds of consideration, and the possible bases of them, to emerge. It's not until the seventeenth century and afterward – for instance in the writings of Clarke, Cumberland, and most lucidly Butler, and then also in Price and Reid – that we find this idea clearly formulated. Then Kant gave a substantial philosophical explanation of it.

Much of the difficulty articulating the conflict arose because of well-entrenched features of Christian doctrine. From the standpoint of these ideas, it's not at all clear that the notion of a conflict between duty and interest makes sense. Much standard Christian theology works, indeed, against the whole idea that the conflict can arise.

We need to start with one of the most important ideas in Christian ethics, the so-called Golden Rule. It brings us very close to the idea of a possible conflict but not quite to it, or at least not at all unmistakably.

Two of the biblical formulations of the Golden Rule are these:

And as ye would that men should do to you, do ye also to them likewise. (Luke 6: 31)

and

Therefore all things whatsoever ye would that men should do to you, do ye even so to them. (Matthew 7: 12)

As is widely noted, sayings like these could be taken not as expressing a notion of moral obligation as distinct from one's own happiness, but as straightforwardly egoistic. Thus it would be tantamount to: "Don't do things that make others unhappy because they may retaliate against you and make you unhappy; instead, do things to make them happy because that will increase the chances that they'll reciprocate." Formulations like these could help make it harder to think of the Golden Rule as expressing the possibility of the relevant conflict. For they can leave open that one's own well-being is the only relevant practical consideration.

However, the Golden Rule also has a non-egoistic interpretation, of course. It's espoused by those who place the Rule in the context of this injunction:

> Love your enemies, do good to them which hate you, bless them that curse you, and pray for them which despitefully use you. (Luke 6: 27–8)

But even statements like this, if one's not careful to explore alternative construals of it, can be taken in a self-regarding way. What's needed to block such an interpretation, and to bring out the idea of the conflict clearly, is a baldly explicit statement that a person's own ultimate good can clash with the norm of love of neighbor or of humankind. Such a statement, of course, isn't made here.

Greek thought was acquainted with a non-egoist understanding of the idea of the Golden Rule. It comes to light, for instance, in the historian Herodotus. He recounts the following story. After the tyrant Polycrates of Samos dies, the man to whom his power has passed speaks as follows:

> [T]he scepter of Polycrates and the power it represents have passed into my hands. So I may, if I wish, become your absolute master. As far as I am able, however, I shall refrain from doing myself what I would rebuke in another. I did not approve of the conduct of Polycrates, and I would not approve the conduct of any other man who sought power over people as good as himself; therefore, now that Polycrates has met his end, I intend to surrender power, and to proclaim you equal before the law. (Herodotus, *History*, III.142)

The idea here could be expressed in the injunction,

> Don't do unto others what you'd disapprove of their doing to you, and do unto others what you'd approve of their doing to you.

This presents the possibility of two distinct attitudes: what you'd want to do or be done, and what you'd *approve* or *disapprove* of. The latter could be taken in a moral sense, and would then make room for a conflict between morality and what one wants.

Even though such a formulation of the Golden Rule makes the possibility of conflict clear, and even though the conflict seems evident in much philosophical and popular thought, nevertheless the conflict wasn't easy to articulate within the context of Christian philosophy.

This topic is a complicated one to pick one's way through. Intertwined with it are questions about free will, responsibility, and about divine foreknowledge and omnipotence and beneficence, along with Aquinas' idea of the "collaboration" of free will and grace; all these run well beyond the present topic.

On a standard Christian view, what's right is defined and constituted by the law of God, whether created by his will or apprehended by his understanding (and perhaps also, on some views, the understanding of an individual human being). That's definitive of right action and righteous living.

How, though, can we imagine a person facing an opposition between such a course, on the one hand, and his greatest happiness on the other? How, in other words, could we picture a person as saying to himself, "One course will lead to my greatest well-being, and the other conforms to morality, and I must choose which to follow"? There seem to be two standard Christian views to take, but neither allows that conflict to arise.

On one view, salvation and so one's ultimate happiness is achieved through one's works, i.e., what one does. But to reach this result requires being rewarded by God, just exactly as not reaching it requires being punished by him. But God's reward will come only to the righteous and his punishment only to the unrighteous. God can't be expected to make mistakes about this matter. So on this view one can't reasonably think oneself to be deliberating about a choice between considerations of morality and those of one's own ultimate well-being. You know that if your happiness is affected by your decision, then it's guaranteed that you'll be happy if and only if you choose righteousness.

On the other view, salvation comes through divine grace and divine grace alone. If that's so, then righteous choices don't guarantee salvation. That is, a person might choose righteousness, but still not ultimately be happy. However, that can't present a conflict that can be taken account of in an individual's deliberation, because it doesn't depend on him, but rather on God and his granting of grace. Therefore, on this view, the individual can't *choose* salvation, or for that matter anything that would definitely bring it about, or even cause its probability to go up (any more than one could, for example, deliberate about or choose whether the number of stars shall be even or odd). But since the person can't bring about or influence the giving of grace, the individual can't deliberate at all about his well-being in the long term.

It's therefore no wonder that, as Sidgwick saw, the Christian tradition didn't arrive at an entirely sharp posing of the conflict between obligation and one's own happiness until the seventeenth century, although it sensed the tension existed all along. The conflict emerged gradually, in the writings especially of the philosophers Cumberland, Clarke, and Butler. Then an elaborate philosophical account of how it was possible was offered by Kant.

Pre-Kantian Modern Articulations of the Conflict

Although Kant was the first to construct an elaborate account, motivated by broad philosophical considerations, of how morality could be rationally binding even if it doesn't bring happiness, essential parts of the Kantian scheme had already been conceived and deployed.

Henry More (1614–87), for instance, espouses a principle of benevolence according to which if it be good that one man should be supplied with the means of living well and happily, it is mathematically certain that it is doubly good that two should be so supplied, and so on. (quoted in Sidgwick, *Outlines of the History of Ethics*, pp. 169–75)

It doesn't take much mathematics to note that where one's own happiness clashes with the happiness of two other people, this statement implies that their happiness is twice as good as one's own. More doesn't always adhere to this inference, however, and so a deliberative conflict between altruism and one's own happiness is left somewhat obscure.

A move in the same direction is made by Richard Cumberland (1632–1718). He is famous for anticipating, in an approximate way, utilitarianism, with his claim that "the common good of all" is the end to which all standards are to be assessed. He maintains, moreover, that

the greatest possible benevolence of every rational agent towards all the rest constitutes the happiest state of each and all, so far as depends on their own power, and is necessarily required for their happiness; accordingly the common good will be the supreme law. (Ibid.)

It's unclear here (as it also is in Mill) how the happiness of all comes to be a reason for a particular individual, but there's no doubt that Cumberland wished to say that it is.

Samuel Clarke (1675–1729) took an even more noticeable step towards the conclusion that Kant elaborated. In the first place, he explicitly tried to show that moral duties are incumbent on a person independent of the rewards and punishments prescribed by God – though he did maintain that those are certain. Secondly, he maintained that a greater good is to be preferred to a lesser one, regardless of whether the good is one's own or another's. Moreover he contended that this thesis has the same status as a mathematical axiom.

Others as well, such as Joseph Butler (1692–1752) and Francis Hutcheson (1694–1747) drew a clear distinction between those rational considerations that bear on one's own well-being, or self-love, and those that are universal in pertaining to the happiness of others in general. The more clearly it came to be said that people naturally have benevolent feeling toward others, not only affection for their own pleasures, the easier it was to realize, as Butler unambiguously does, that these can oppose each other.

This realization is also pursued by Shaftesbury (1671–1713), Richard Price (1723–91), Thomas Reid (1710–96), and Adam Smith (1723–90). Price makes a couple of especially noteworthy claims. One is that moral demands don't arise only from benevolence toward one's fellow human beings (which of course was already present in the biblical injunction to "love thine enemy"). Moral demands arise also from other principles, such as a principle of truth-telling.

Price's other, even more significant, thesis, taking him further in the direction of Kant, goes beyond the statement that there are grounds for obeying morality that are independent of its conduciveness to one's own well-being. This is the thesis that adhering to morality out of a desire for one's well-being is precisely the *wrong* sort of motivation for a morally upright person to have. As Sidgwick stressed, this thesis had always figured in Christian thought, and it was to be central to Kant's outlook. (It's also to be interpreted, I think, as an echo of Aristotle's view that morally virtuous actions are to be regarded as worth doing "for their own sake.")

Shaftesbury has something even more striking to say on this topic. Taking into account the Christian view that God punishes wrongdoing and rewards righteousness, he insists that nevertheless the reason to do right isn't simply that otherwise God will punish you. Rather, you should already be moved by the fact that the action is right, and register that God will reward it for that reason. And he carries this thought to the point of maintaining that you'd take the right act to be obligatory *even if* you didn't believe that it would be rewarded. Thus:

> whoever has a firm belief of a god whom he does merely call good
> but of whom in reality he believes nothing beside real good . . . such

a person, believing rewards or retributions in another life, must believe them annexed to real goodness and merit, real villainy and baseness, and not to any accidental qualities or circumstances, in which respect they cannot properly be styled rewards or punishments, but capricious distributions of happiness or unhappiness to creatures. These are the only terms on which the belief of a world to come can happily influence the believer. And on these terms, and by virtue of this belief, man perhaps may retain his virtue and integrity, even under the hardest thoughts of human nature, when either by any ill circumstance or untoward doctrine he is brought to that unfortunate opinion of 'virtue's being naturally an enemy to happiness in life'. (*Characteristics of Men . . .* , pp. 189–90)

The Kantian Articulation of the Conflict

To arrive with full clarity at the view that a person may be faced with a choice between adhering to moral or altruistic norms and pursuing his own happiness, certain ideas have to be deployed in a particular way. Though the requisite thoughts certainly existed before Kant – indeed, in Aristotle and especially Plato – only in Kant's writings were they developed and argued for as fully and broadly as they need to be to make the conflict unmistakable.

The most important move that Kant made in this regard was to set up an elaborate schema of philosophical explanation and justification of the idea that an obligation might be rationally binding quite *independently of the expectation of rewards* for righteousness and punishment for unrighteousness. That is, he tried to answer the question, "Why would a person deliberately do something that he ought to do if he doesn't want to?"

Kant's response is constructed on a basis of complex philosophical reflection on the nature of human thought and action and, above all, the "will." He tries to show what could persuade a person to will to do what's obligatory in spite of his desire or inclination to do something else. The depth and ingenuity of his proposal – quite apart from whether it's adequate – forced all subsequent thinkers to take it seriously. It was henceforth impossible simply to brush off the idea that the binding character of morality might arise from something quite separate from one's concern with one's happiness.

Kant's schema was constructed with the idea of the so-called *Categorical Imperative.* In its chief formulation, this is: "Act only according to that maxim whereby you can at the same time will that it should become a universal law." This embodies the idea that it's *rational* to adhere to morality, out of "respect" for the "moral law." It's not because of any expectation of consequences favorable to one's own happiness (or indeed anyone else's). The Categorical Imperative is thus designed to provide an entirely non-self-regarding explanation of a person's regarding moral norms as binding. (A further feature of the explanation is that it ascribes "autonomy" to the person; see Schneewind 1998.)

In this way the binding character of moral norms becomes sharply distinguished, in Kant's view, from the aim of one's happiness. One can place the considerations for doing something into two separate baskets: "Will it be conducive to my happiness?" and "Am I morally obligated (or permitted, or forbidden) to do it?" Not only is one's happiness not a part of the reason for adhering to morality; the Categorical Imperative provides the reason for adhering to morality with a far more substantial and complex articulation than had ever existed theretofore.

Kant even goes so far as to contend, especially in the *Grounding for the Metaphysics of Morals,* that the properly moral reason to adhere to one's obligations mustn't include any consideration of happiness *at all.* Rather moral reasons arise entirely from the Categorical Imperative itself, via what Kant calls "respect for the moral law." This contention highlights (without actually adding logically to it) the independence of moral considerations from self-regarding ones in which happiness figures.

The aim of one's own happiness is thus acknowledged to lead a person wherever it contingently happens to. It's capable of leading someone to choose actions that contravene morality. Moreover a person can believe that that will happen, and thus be faced with a deliberative conflict, over whether to follow his duty or to pursue his happiness.

In one respect Kant has departed, for purposes of this philosophical account, from the standard Christian position. The certainty of actual rewards for righteousness and punishment for moral transgressions has dropped out of his picture. That means that consideration of one's happiness, through God's rewards, is no part of moral motivation, though Shaftesbury had already taken the same step quite a bit earlier (see above).

Kant thus tried to explain why a person could choose to do what's moral even when it works against his desires or his happiness. At the same time he also insisted on the specifically moral character of praise and blame. On his view, it's an entirely different matter from the evaluation of any other sort of thing. It's a very different matter, too, from the kind of congratulations that one might offer to a person who's happy. Kant treated *that* as similar to the congratulations that come to a person who's won the lottery or had some other stroke of good fortune, or for that matter to a cat that has swallowed a canary.

It hadn't proved easy to describe moral judgments as *sui generis*. Hume had tried it by speaking of "approbation." Smith complained that on Hume's account, our favorable attitude towards a person's moral conduct turns out to be no different from the favorable view that one might take of "a chest of drawers." Both attitudes, taking Hume's view, were provoked by the fact that both things are "agreeable." Smith and Kant exerted themselves to show that these are two quite different matters. Smith focused on social context. Kant turned to metaphysics, attempting to show why a person is the very special sort of thing to which a special sort of attitude, moral praise and blame, can be appropriate.

For an investigation into the history of happiness it's of particular interest to know exactly in what sense Kant thought that we fail to grasp the concept of it. He must have believed that we have some understanding of it, at least in some respects.

As I said in Chapter 4, Kant holds in the *Grounding* that:

> [M]en cannot form any definite and certain concept of the sum of satisfaction of all inclinations that is called happiness. (399)

That might seem to bar us from making any reasoned judgments involving the concept of happiness. However, Kant doesn't seem to want to go that far. For he also says that it's fitting for a person's moral virtue to be rewarded by happiness. To repeat another passage, from the *Critique of Practical Reason*:

> inasmuch as virtue and happiness together constitute the possession of the highest good for one person, and happiness in exact proportion to morality (as the worth of a person and his worthiness to be happy) constitutes the highest good of a possible world. . . . (Bk II, ch. ii)

Obviously we must have *some* grasp of the concept of happiness, of the sort needed to make this judgment involving it.

But although Kant believes that we do have that degree or type of understanding of the concept of happiness, his statement that we don't have a "definite and certain concept of the sum of satisfaction of all inclinations" has to be taken into account. How, according to Kant, can we grasp the idea that there can be conflicts between happiness and moral obligation if we don't have a "definite and certain concept" of happiness?

The answer is this. When Kant is emphasizing the deficiency of our understanding of the notion of happiness, he tends to picture the conflict this way. It's not conceived as a conflict between obligation and happiness, but rather as being between obligation and a *particular* inclination or desire. In that case we shouldn't think of him as believing that there's a conflict between obligation and *happiness*. Or at least we shouldn't put it that way if it would suggest that we have a well-defined notion of happiness as the sum of satisfactions, to set against the notion of obligation. Rather, we have an "indefinite and uncertain" concept of satisfactions that we might have. When we observe a conflict between (what we loosely call) happiness and duty, we're focusing on a particular one of them and seeing that it opposes an obligation that we're under.

Other thinkers – those who didn't agree with Kant that our grasp of the concept of happiness is so indefinite – were in a position to say roundly that there's a conflict between, say, duty and (self-)interest or the like. That's the form in which the problem has for the most part been set in English-language philosophy since Kant's time.

Plato and Kant Compared

Plato is the only philosopher before Kant who seems to me to have offered anything approaching Kant's characterization of universal practical rationality. Plato's account isn't as elaborate as Kant's, but it's the only one comparable to it.

The problem that we're investigating is twofold. One question is why a person might choose to act rightly against his own self-interest or happiness. That's the question that most philosophers have posed over the last century or so. The other question is why a person would choose to act rightly against what he desired or wanted. As just explained, Kant's formulations tend toward posing the latter question, because he takes talk of "happiness" to involve a concept that isn't "definite" for us.

Plato poses both questions separately from each other. In his *Gorgias* he confronts opponents, especially Gorgias and Callicles, who think that a person's best off if he does whatever he wants at the time. Accordingly Plato tries to show that it can make sense to act against what one wants at the time to do. Plato draws out the admission that Callicles in fact has the desire to control some of his own immediate desires, and is willing to accept the idea of planning for future satisfactions, and for other things.

In *Republic* I, on the other hand, the main opponent, Thrasymachus, is someone who talks the language of "advantage" and "benefit," and who attacks justice for being "another's good," i.e., for involving a sacrifice of one's own well-being. Plato responds in two ways. First, he argues that a person's happiness is enhanced by justice to a far greater extent than Thrasymachus recognizes. Second, however, Plato also argues that in his ideal city, the rulers must be prepared to govern their city, even though there's "a way of life that's better than ruling for those who are to rule" (521a). That way of life is philosophy, which the rulers would, according to Plato, much prefer to the toilsome business of governing. However, they choose to govern. That is, they choose to govern even though they'll thereby incur some sacrifice of their happiness. (Plato thinks, however, that they're extremely happy anyway, happier than anyone else.)

Like Kant, Plato accepts the challenge of trying to explain why anyone would choose to sacrifice any satisfaction or happiness in order to do what's right or just. The details of these explanations are beyond the scope of this book. Very briefly, however, we can say this. Kant believes that universal moral laws are accepted by reason, and indeed in a sense legislated by reason for itself, as the basis for its choices. To make a long story very short, it is the *universality* of moral laws that makes reason accept them as binding.

Plato has a different explanation: much less elaborate, and without reliance on the special kind of universality that Kant links to the notion of reason. What plays the role in Plato that universality plays for Kant is the notion of the real *function* of a type of thing. In Plato's view, reason accepts the idea that a thing has a determinate function or natural task. The function of a city is to enable human beings to live and to live well. Within a city, the function of a ruler is to govern. It's the recognition of this function that persuades the ruler, Plato believes, that governing is the thing to do, in spite of the sacrifice of happiness that it entails.

It seems fair to say that at least in modern times, Kant's response to the problem has attracted more adherents than Plato's has. (Plato's response is taken over by Aristotle, however, and his version has had a wide following; see Chapter 7.) The point to stress, however, is that both of them are attempts to respond to just the same problem, or pair of problems: how a person might reasonably choose to act against his desire or, alternatively, his conception of his own good. It remains to consider some of the implications of this point.

Reactions to Kant and to the Conflict

Consider now how the concept of happiness looks in the aftermath of Kant's work. One reaction to Kant's overall view is to accept it. If one does that, then one acknowledges that although we're aware of inclinations whose fulfillment is part of happiness, we don't have any clear concept of happiness itself, because there isn't one (see Chapter 7). The search for a coherent way to take all aims, etc., into consideration is abandoned.

Another possible thing to do is simply to reject Kantian arguments and hold to the old egoist position, the sort that Thrasymachus espoused in Book I of Plato's *Republic*. That means saying that the basis of all decisions is the furthering of one's own happiness. That, unlike Kant's view, might require having some clear conception of what one's happiness is.

Another reaction to Kant's thinking is to accept only part of it. One can agree that he'd shown why it's rational to conform to morality, but deny his claim that we don't have a concept of our own well-being. That could leave us with two distinct and divergent standards of rationality for deciding what to do and how to be. We'd then face what Sidgwick near the beginning of the twentieth century called "the dualism of practical reason."

The "dualism of practical reason" expresses the idea that there are two ways of making choices or decisions that come under the heading "Reason," one egoist and the other universal. The one aims at one's own good, while the other aims at some kind of universality. Sidgwick himself takes the essence of the dualism to be the opposition of one's own good and the utilitarian good of all. (He doesn't think that Kant's view is ultimately defensible, and he's not satisfied with, for example, the British Moralists' undefined "general good" or the "well-being of all."

Sidgwick thought the dualism of practical reason was disastrous. One's well-being and obedience to moral standards could be two diverging paths, so that one would have to make a decision between them. What worried Sidgwick was the idea that *reason*, or something that could properly be called by that name, might be on both sides. The notion of practical rationality would be split into two.

If no way could be found to adjudicate between the two ways of arriving at decisions, practical reason would be forever paralyzed, caught between two equally authoritative and convincing sorts of consideration, like Buridan's ass between two piles of hay equidistant from its mouth, and with no motivation to go for one or the other. Once thinkers came to talk in this way, the idea of the conflict of one's happiness and morality had been brought fully into the open.

Someone could also respond to Kant's arguments by denying that they're able to establish a distinction between obligation and any form of well-being. For instance one can contend that a full comprehension of these two concepts shows any conflict between them to be illusory. One such option is "fusionist": to argue that moral virtue and one's well-being are actually identical. This paradoxical-seeming view, as noted, was espoused by the Stoics. Occasionally Hegel seems to advocate the same view. It's also followed by some "communitarian" thought.

For most thinkers who follow this path, the circle of people to whom someone's morally bound doesn't include all humanity or all rational beings, as Kant thought, but rather the members of one's community. After all, it's much more appealing to identify one's happiness with the happiness of a relatively small group or social unit than with that of everyone, unless one can picture the whole world as a community.

Less extreme and more popular than this fusion of morality and interest is an "inclusivist" position. This strategy too can be found in

Hegel, and in some neo-Hegelians such as T. H. Green, and similar ideas had appeared in Butler and Hutcheson. Inclusivism says that happiness is a capacious enough concept to "include" morality itself. Thus your being happy might be claimed to include your conformity to moral norms; that is, simply the fact that you conform to them, not the feelings or thoughts that result from your doing so. Your happiness might also, on the same conception, include the well-being of other people (once again, your happiness would include the fact of their well-being itself, not just the feelings in you that that might cause). (Like fusionists, adherents of inclusivism usually narrow the circle of moral obligations to cover a community rather than all humanity.)

A different but related strategy is adopted by Foot. She argues for a distinction between "happiness" and what she calls "deep happiness." If one objects, as she does, to the thought that a person might be a viciously sadistic concentration-camp guard and nevertheless have a happy life, Foot suggests that such a person, even if out of perversion he experiences jolly feelings, can at least be held not to possess *deep* happiness. Deep happiness is thus a morally tinged happiness. That's somewhat like the inclusivist strategy of saying that happiness includes moral components.

As this book has taken pains to stress, saying that happiness has certain components doesn't yet tell us what roles they play in the overall complex of considerations that make it up. A given consideration might be very important, or very minor, or important in some situations and not in others, and so on.

Inclusivism has a difficulty to face on this account. By itself, it doesn't provide a substantial reconciliation of happiness with morality after all. Thus if your happiness includes a plurality of parts, of which two are the well-being of others and one is adherence to morality, then the possibility can't be ruled out that these two parts will conflict with the others. If your physical comfort is one of those other parts, then you seemingly could have a conflict between your comfort and fulfilling your moral obligations. As in all such cases of conflict within happiness, some other considerations will have to decide which to pursue more.

An inclusivist view wouldn't call this a conflict between your obligations and your happiness. Rather, inclusivism would see here a conflict between two *parts of happiness*. In effect, though, the conflict seems to come to the same thing – the difference being merely terminological.

Looking back at Aristotle, one can see that he was in the same position. He presents a conflict between devoting yourself to politics and excellence of character and devoting yourself to philosophical thought. The conflict shows itself in his terminology as one between two kinds or aspects of happiness. Another way of talking would have been possible too. Since excellence of character is largely other-regarding, since it benefits one's fellow-citizens, and contemplation isn't, one could think of the conflict as one between one's civic duty and one's own private benefit. Again it's not clear that the difference between these two ways of describing the conflict is more than one of labels.

The Fragmentation of the Concept?

The historical results of Kant's thinking for the treatment of the concept of happiness have been substantial. One is the aforementioned attempt, of fusionists and inclusivists, to appeal to Greek ethics of the classical period, and in particular Plato and Aristotle. Hegel led this effort. It marked a break with the previous two centuries, during which classical Greek ethics had been relatively neglected, and philosophers and other readers had paid attention mostly to Roman philosophy and, through it, to Greek philosophy of the Hellenistic period.

A different sort of result of Kant's thinking has been subtler and less explicit. It has to do with the sense that terms like "happiness," "well-being," etc. allude to a single, all-inclusive measure of evaluation of a person's condition or life.

This conception of a single measure of well-being has always been under pressure, as I've said, from the rival view that one's obligations can clash with one's happiness. As long as performance or non-performance of one's obligations can have repercussions for the evaluation of one's condition – whether one's "virtuous" or not, for instance – there's a possibility that there will be two independent schemes or "scores" for assessing how well one's doing and how good one's life is.

If the evaluation of a person's condition can split into two evaluations – happiness and morality – then why not into more? The question is thus raised whether, in general, there's any particular reason to suppose that there should be or can be a single, all-in measure of a person's condition. Metaphorically, once a fissure opens between the gauging of someone's happiness and the moral evaluation of his condition, it starts to look possible that more cracks will open – as the existence of other terms of assessment like "perfection" might already have indicated. If there can be a conflict between moral assessment and a non-moral one, why should it be surprising if there are other conflicts too?

Or one might ask, once the gap between duty and happiness has opened, whether the idea of a single overall assessment of a human being's condition of life might not itself simply be a mistake. Perhaps, after all, there's no intelligible way of making such an overall assessment. Already in an earlier chapter weighty considerations made evident how difficult such an overall assessment would be to construct (Chapter 2). Now in this chapter we've focused on the evident gap between two distinct types of evaluations, the moral ones and the others, which may well be unbridgeable. All the more reason to ask whether a single all-inclusive assessment of a person's condition is possible. That's an issue to be explored further (see Chapter 7).

Chapter 6

Happiness, Fact, and Value

Discovering Happiness

Here's a question you might ask about happiness. Although it hasn't been prominent in the history of the concept, it's relevant to some of the important issues.

Can two people widely differing in moral values and other beliefs determine in common, or come to agreement, about whether any given person is happy? Or will their differences over morals and other values so affect their conceptions of happiness, and their respective ways of trying to determine whether it attaches to someone, as to undermine their attempts together to find out how happy or unhappy someone is?

We could also ask whether it's a *fact* that someone is happy and to what degree, or, on the other hand, whether saying that someone's happy or not is "value-laden." This latter question is subject to the common complaint that there's no clear actual distinction between values and facts. Despite this, let's try to understand the question, for present purposes, at face value. So we're asking whether disagreements about moral and other values will affect our attempts to determine whether and to what degree someone is happy.

We can also ask a historical question, closely linked to the one just posed: whether there are cases in the history of happiness in which two philosophers holding widely differing ethical views nevertheless agreed what happiness is. If this did happen, then those two philosophers might try to discover in some straightforward way (or expect others to do so) which of their ethical views, if held by a person, would lead him to be happier. One of them would say to the general public, "Go and try it! You'll see that if you accept my view, then you'll be happier." And the other would issue the same advertisement. And they'd both expect the answer to emerge from these tests by consumers. The answer to this question is: there have indeed been such cases. I'll describe one case shortly, from the Hellenistic period of Greek philosophy.

Another historical question, a broader one. As the concept of happiness has developed, have people (or, philosophers) treated happiness as the kind of thing whose presence could be determined in the rough sort of way that this kind of test presupposes? Or not? Have people believed that anyone with a normal familiarity with the world can determine this, regardless of what values he holds – in the way that any normal person, with whatever moral views, can determine who weighs 20 kilograms? Or have people believed that to determine how happy someone is you have to have the correct moral position yourself?

The answer to this question is that philosophers, at any rate, have been divided about it. The issue is a bit murky, because philosophers haven't often spoken of the issue explicitly. Nevertheless some philosophers seem to have assumed this: happiness is something that anyone, no matter what his values, can detect in himself or another person. And other philosophers seem, at least implicitly, to have held the contrary.

Here's a reason to expect a lot of disagreement, among both philosophers and others, about who's happy and to what degree. If happiness takes account of a whole range of aims, and if we don't have a clear idea of how, if at all, they're to be organized or integrated into a good condition, different people will have widely diverging views about *that*. But if people disagree about that, they're almost certainly going to have trouble agreeing about who's happy and how happy they are.

Some Agreement about Happiness and Some Disagreement

We'd like to find in the history of philosophy some progress, at least, towards a coherent, unified concept of happiness. It may be that each individual philosopher's approach falls short of that goal. But even if that's so, perhaps the sum total of such efforts, surveyed in their historical sequence, might show us where the goal lies, and enable us to extrapolate to see how to reach it.

Perhaps some cause for optimism can be found in the historical periods when some consensus has prevailed about certain important features of happiness. There have in fact been such periods, sometimes fairly long ones. True, a consensus can break up quickly once pressure is put on it. Still, it's worth looking at the conditions under which consensus obtains.

Here's what seems to be a case in point. In the Hellenistic period and into the period of the Roman republic and the Roman empire, there was fairly widespread agreement that happiness, or a crucial component of it, consisted in a kind of *tranquillity*, or at least freedom from certain sorts of cares and anxieties. On this the practical philosophy of Stoicism, Epicureanism, and Skepticism shows a relatively high degree of consensus. Stoics, Epicureans, and Skeptics could put out rival advertisements. Each often claimed that if its views were adopted, people would be more tranquil and therefore happier. That gave them something approaching a neutral measure of the acceptability of their respective theories. That illustrates the way in which happiness has been taken by some to be a neutral measure of how good a person's condition is.

Consensus on this point held even though these doctrines differ greatly on what this freedom from tranquillity itself consists in, and on how it is, or ought to be, attained. Epicurus believed that it's a form of pleasure, consisting in the absence of pain and anxiety. The Stoics took tranquillity to involve the view that the contingent events of life are indifferent, and as inevitable and necessary parts of the cosmic order. The Skeptics, for their part, believed that tranquillity arises from a skeptical attitude toward all issues about value. All three schools thought that they could all recognize who was tranquil, and that terms like "tranquillity" and "freedom from disturbance" could be used to characterize the optimal state of a person. What they mainly disagreed about was how a person could most effectively be brought to such a state.

Each of the three schools advertised itself on the basis of its own strategy for achieving tranquillity. That doesn't mean, though, that they took the truth or acceptability of their doctrines to consist simply in their respective capacity to have this effect. Their doctrines weren't in that sense pragmatically justified or interpreted. They competed with each other in "the marketplace of ideas" (in Mill's phrase) on these terms.

On the whole it appears that the Stoics came out best in this competition for adherents. Moreover there's a certain psychological plausibility in the idea that they should have done so. Although the Epicureans maintained that what they meant by "pleasure" was a condition that would be free from disturbance, the association with the usual meaning of the term, with its connotation of physical pleasure, was too strong for that idea to be generally accepted (though of course that connotation itself no doubt attracted some people for reasons having nothing to do with tranquillity, but rather with its opposite).

The claims of Skepticism to bring tranquillity seemed, and still seem, particularly weak. The urge to reach certainty about some things is best put aside. But not about everything. As many have noted, there are matters that people really don't like to feel unsure about. The thought of not knowing how they really are doesn't make most people tranquil; rather, it makes them nervous. Given this fact the Skeptical strategy for happiness couldn't win wide acceptance.

The Hellenistic period isn't the only period that saw a consensus about some characteristics of happiness. Other times and places have seen a similar phenomenon. We could cite seventeenth-century

France, for instance, for a predominant hedonism among some social classes. Under those circumstances the relevant debates would be about what sort of pleasure might be most stably maintained. And of course Christianity established some agreement about what an optimal state of a human being would be. Aquinas' conception of perfect human happiness as the vision of the divine essence, for instance, could be widely accepted within the Roman Catholic Church.

On the other hand, though, there have been plenty of periods at which these sorts of consensus have been lacking, and at which disagreements seem almost unbridgeable. The writings of Plato are witness to such controversies, between Plato himself on the one hand and some of the Sophists on the other. Aristotle, too, describes similar differences of opinion.

Plato maintains throughout his works, and notably in the *Republic*, that the announced views of his opponents exhibit a nearly complete misconception of what a good condition of a human being is. Many of those opponents take external appearances at face value, Plato says. They "judge from outside, as a child does, who's dazzled by the façade that tyrants adopt for those outside them to see" (577a).

They therefore form the misguided view that a ruling tyrant is the happiest of human beings. Plato holds that his opponents are looking in entirely the wrong place. If we saw what's going on in a tyrant's soul, he says, we'd realize that he isn't happy at all, and that happiness isn't what he thinks it is.

Plato seems sure, on the one hand, that he could persuade basically sensible people like his interlocutors, Glaucon and Adeimantus, that the tyrant isn't happy. But does he believe that he could ever persuade the tyrant himself of this? Does he think that his character Thrasymachus, his adversary in *Republic* I, could be convinced of it? That's an interesting and difficult question. It's hard to say to what extent Plato thought that he could find common ground with such opponents, or show them what they'd regard as sufficient reasons to accept his view. But some interpreters are sure that Thrasymachus could never be rationally persuaded that it makes sense for someone to be just if it were possible to get away with being unjust.

Unquestionably Plato doesn't think that finding common ground would be easy. It seems to me likely that in Plato's opinion, *if* you could get Thrasymachus to sit still long enough and listen, then he'd be convinced that his conception was incoherent by his own standards. But as a point of interpretation of the *Republic* this question isn't easy to settle definitively. What does Plato think it would take to get a thoroughly tyrannical personality to sit down and listen? Maybe the cause of his recalcitrance is that he wouldn't do that. And maybe that's supposed to be so because he doesn't see the point of doing that. So perhaps Plato thinks that this is in some sense an irreconcilable disagreement.

Now look at Aristotle. Although his view of happiness diverges less from ordinary conceptions of it than Plato's does, he joins Plato in believing that many people are radically mistaken about what it is. Aristotle believes, too, that identification of the human good requires an investigation that goes beyond ordinary views, even though it starts from them. He also maintains that only a person who's been well raised in good habits can profit from lectures on ethics. He's apparently not prepared to try to convince just anybody who happens to walk into his lecture hall. And perhaps that's so because he doesn't think that everyone can be convinced by reasonable ethical arguments.

Looking back to the partial consensus that existed in the Hellenistic period, moreover, one has to acknowledge that it was sharply limited. Not everyone agrees that happiness is tranquillity, or even that tranquillity is an especially important part of it. Nietzsche doesn't, for instance. Neither do Aristippus or Bentham. Aristotle doesn't agree completely. And on the other hand not everyone agrees that happiness is pleasure or that it essentially involves pleasure. The view is even attributed to Plato's nephew, and successor as head of the Academy, that pleasure is bad – even though Aristotle dismisses this thesis as absurd.

Empiricism, Science, and Policy

In the face of these levels of dissent about what happiness is, we can look for consensus on something else: a *method* or *approach* to the investigation, on which we might come to agreement.

It's hard to find clear views about this matter early on. A striking fact about the history of the concept is the absence of discussion of what would support an account of happiness. People say what they think it is, and they give arguments for their views, but the arguments often have an ad hoc look. They start *in medias res*, without much consideration of the appropriate method. Perhaps that's to the good. Perhaps there's no appropriate method for settling this issue. But in any case, philosophers talk a good deal less about the way to explicate the concept of happiness than they do about the explication of other sorts of concepts, such as goodness.

One way of investigating happiness, however, has consistently won adherents. People readily think of happiness as something that's connected in an observably regular way with what happens to people and how they behave. Empirical observation, it seems, ought to be able to tell us something about the circumstances in which people are happy, and what being happy will make them do. That would make happiness into an empirical concept, or enough of one for empirical investigation and science to study and identify.

Once again the Hellenistic period exhibits consensus. Stoics and Epicureans were empiricists in the theory of knowledge. They both make essentially empiricist arguments on behalf of their accounts of the optimal human state. The arguments rest on the observation of infants. The thought is that society can induce people to adopt conventionally supported views of happiness, but that if we observe human beings before society has imposed its views on them, we can see what they really aim at. Babies, the Epicureans believed, aim at pleasure in the Epicurean sense (see Chapter 3). That seemed to them like an argument for hedonism. The Stoics believed that they aim at self-preservation and an "appropriation" (*oikeiôsis*) to themselves of things around them that would preserve their existence. The Stoics took that to support their view that the end for a human being was "living consistently with nature."

The pertinent fact here isn't the particular views that the Stoics and Epicureans respectively defended, but the fact that they both tried to defend their views through observation of a type of human behavior. What they ended up jointly demonstrating, however, was how hard it is to find empirical observations that settle this issue.

Although after the Hellenistic period there was a long hiatus in the tradition of trying to use empirical observation systematically to discover the nature of happiness, the tradition started up again later. The most instructive heir to it, it seems to me, was Mill. Given the state of the ethical discussions in which he found himself in the nineteenth century, it made sense for him to deplore the disagreement that both then prevailed and had, seen from his standpoint, prevailed over the ages. I've already quoted this passage:

> From the dawn of philosophy, the question concerning the *summum bonum*, or, what is the same thing, concerning the foundation of morality, has been accounted the main problem in speculative thought, has occupied the most gifted intellects and divided them into sects and schools. . . . And after more than two thousand years the same discussions continue . . . and neither thinkers nor mankind at large seem nearer to being unanimous on the subject, than when the youth Socrates listened to the old Protagoras. . . . (*Utilitarianism*, ch. 1)

Mill hoped to be able to change this situation through the general acceptance of utilitarianism.

In part Mill's efforts took the same form as those of many other thinkers – by no means all – in the nineteenth century and since. Following Bentham, Mill contended that doing what's right consists in doing that which will produce the greatest happiness of the greatest number. That idea has been a powerful force in ethics – Cumberland, for instance, had been an early advocate of a position that was in effect utilitarian – but Mill never had reason to take for granted that it would persuade everyone. In fact he knew that he had an uphill fight.

Mill was aware, in particular, that people might well not accept the thesis that justice – a significant component of the right – consists simply in increasing the amount of happiness in the world (*Utilitarianism*, ch. 5). In all ages of speculation one of the strongest obstacles to the reception of the doctrine that utility or happiness is the criterion of right and wrong has been drawn from the idea of justice.

The cause of the special obstacle that justice poses to utilitarianism is that according to the ordinary ethical outlook, justice seems clearly to be not simply a matter of producing happiness, but also of its distribution. If happiness is increased but the increase goes only to a few, then that situation is prima facie unjust. The fact of that injustice, it seems pretty evident, counts against the thesis that right action is simply the action by which happiness is produced.

So when Mill argued in chapter 5 of *Utilitarianism* that his doctrine can in fact accommodate the ordinary outlook on ethics, including justice, he knew that he had his work cut out for him. It's clear from that chapter, too, that he had no systematic argument to which to appeal to support this part of his doctrine.

The other chief part of Bentham's and Mill's doctrine, though, is its hedonist thesis: that the good is happiness, construed as identical with pleasure (see Chapter 3). Here Mill thought that he had a more powerful argument, namely, the same one that the Epicureans had used: straightforward empirical observation. As an empiricist in his theory of knowledge – and thus as holding that all knowledge is grounded in sense experience or sensory observation – he was comfortable presenting this point of view. Taking a cue from earlier thinkers such as Eudoxus and Epicurus (see Chapter 2), Mill maintained that we can simply observe that each person strives for his own happiness, in the sense of his own pleasure.

In addition, Mill also contended that if we make use of all the empirical knowledge that we can gather, we'll be able in the future to generate more happiness around the world

. . . the standard of morality, which may accordingly be defined 'the rules and precepts for human conduct', by the observance of which an existence such as has been described [i.e., an existence exempt as far as possible from pain, and as rich as possible in enjoyments] might be, to the greatest extent possible, secured to all mankind; and not to them only, but so far as the nature of things admits, to the whole sentient creation. (*Utilitarianism*, ch. 2)

Empirical observation can tell us both that the good for human beings is pleasure, and also how to produce more of it.

The idea that's articulated by Mill is an idea that, in one form or another, appeals to many empiricists: that empirical observation can determine what makes people happy and unhappy, and that this empirical information about what happiness is places us in position to determine how we ought to act.

Mill's project stands early in a long line of modern attempts, reaching up to the present and no doubt into the future too, to attack the question of the nature of happiness with the methods of empirical investigation in the social and natural sciences.

This project exemplifies the empiricist, "naturalist" stance which many thinkers have taken since the nineteenth century. It says – here's the naturalism – that information about nature will tell us what our good is, and through that what we should do; and it says, too – the empiricism – that information about nature is obtainable through, and only through, empirical observations. Add to those ideas the thesis that the scientific study of nature is the vehicle for gathering and organizing those observations, and you have *scientific* (or *scientistic*) *naturalism* about happiness and through it about all of ethics.

The forms that this outlook has taken are too varied to canvass at all fully here, but a couple of examples will make its general character clear. Ever since Darwin's theory of evolution was first known of, attempts have been made to apply it to ethics. Sometimes this is done by trying to identify happiness with "survival value." At other times the importance of individuals' happiness is compared unfavorably with that of "the survival of the fittest," as for example in this passage from Herbert Spencer:

> The poverty of the incapable, the distresses that come upon the imprudent, the starvation of the idle, and those shoulderings aside of the weak by the strong, which leave so many 'in shallows and in miseries', are the decrees of a large, farseeing benevolence. (*Social Statics*, III.25)

Efforts to use evolutionary theory to support ethical theses exhibit a frequent and obvious tendency here to confuse ethical claims with straightforwardly empirical propositions. For instance, the mainly empirical claim that misfortunes afflict imprudent people comes to be confused with the claim that imprudent people in some sense *deserve* their distress, or that there's no reason to try to protect them from it. The suggestion is bolstered by a neglect of the fact that distress comes also to those who are very prudent but very unlucky, and the ignoring of the issue of whether it would be worth trying to do something about that.

Efforts to use evolutionary theory in ethics are often characterized by a confused mixing together of some or all of the following distinct things: conduciveness to happiness, pleasure, individual survival, survival of a group, survival of a species, selective pressure for the continuation or propagation of a trait or piece of behavior, and social pressure encouraging or discouraging a trait or piece of behavior. A little reflection on each case shows that none of these is the same as any of the others. No argument that fails to distinguish them can be reliable.

Even so, it's not hard to understand the long-standing tendency to believe that the happiness of an individual is closely tied up with surviving, and via that with the ability to survive. How could it be otherwise? You can't enjoy anything if you don't survive; that's why so many people believe in life after death, and the Greeks believed that the gods' immortality was crucial to their being happy. You might also be glad that your genetic line has lived on long enough to produce you (not that you were responsible for that). From that itself, nothing *follows* about the appropriateness of any generalized gladness about the survival of your species or any other, let alone of the "fittest" individuals, nor to a belief that your well-being is tied up therewith. Still, a propensity to think that well-being can be accounted for by reference to biological selection lives on vigorously in some (not all) quarters. It's a part of the broader propensity, also vigorous, to believe that natural science can, uncontroversially, settle the question what happiness is.

The view in psychology known as behaviorism provides another example of scientific naturalism about well-being, especially in the middle of the twentieth century. Behaviorists have often stressed the implications of their view for social policy. B. F. Skinner, the behaviorist psychologist, became famous for statements such as:

> The one fact that I would cry from every housetop is this: the Good Life is waiting for us – here and now! . . . At this very moment we have the necessary techniques, both material and psychological, to create a full and satisfying life for everyone. (*Walden Two*, ch. 23)

Skinner's making a strategic proposal that takes for granted that happiness can be detected empirically, and that we can discover empirically how to produce it by behavioral reinforcement. This is the reason why he can claim than we have "techniques" to create a satisfying life. Certainly this idea continues to have a considerable following, even when behaviorism in its cruder forms has been put aside.

There have, in fact, been increasing reasons of policy since the eighteenth century to explore happiness through empirical investigation. This begins as follows. Natural science, including the technology that arises from it, has increasingly been a powerful tool. At the very least it's a powerful way – more powerful than anything that anyone had ever come upon before – for reaching certain sorts of specifiable goals. That fact makes people liable to suppose that it might be equally effective at discovering what the goals of policy are or ought to be.

In addition, we can discern another factor working somewhat in parallel. As things that people want are produced more plentifully, and as the distribution of them becomes more and more feasible, scarcities and uneven distributions come to seem less and less unavoidable and more easily remediable. Inequalities and unfairness thus seem less and less a matter of the unchangeable order of things, and more and more the result of human decisions and efforts. Policies come to be conceived to combat them, in a way that people would rarely have dreamed of before.

As that happens, however, the need for the measurement of equalities and inequalities comes to appear increasingly salient. There wasn't much point during the classical period in Greece in trying to measure the relative degree of poverty in two different areas. No one was going to do anything systematic about it, or not anything that would call for measurement. Certainly philosophers and other thinkers weren't going to interest themselves in such large-scale questions of measurement – as opposed to the small-scale measurements of an individual's pleasure noted in the *Protagoras*.

Well-being is clearly one of the things whose distribution concerns people, and that seems to require the measurement of it. So an interest in the project of measuring well-being for these purposes worldwide is called forth by the recognition that it's possible to make use of the results of such measurements. It begins in a halting way in Europe about two centuries ago, and can be seen in Mill's *Utilitarianism* and the character Mrs Jellyby in Dickens's *Bleak House*. Dickens is disturbed by the fact that his character is more concerned with the well-being of faraway people than of her own family. This was another attack on utilitarianism, with its advocacy of doing what would further the greatest happiness of the greatest number.

Measurement: Happiness and Other Concepts

Nowadays empirical measurement – construed as such – is a pervasive activity, occupying the time of prominent philosophers and economists, among others. It figures crucially in ethical doctrines beyond the utilitarianism that first raised interest in it. For instance, John Rawls's theory of justice requires the ability to determine who in society is the "least well off," and the taking of certain measures to raise their level of well-being. As the possibilities of measurement expand, the pressure increases – beyond anything that Plato could have foreseen when he wrote the *Protagoras* – to understand how to carry it out by means of good empirical evidence. For many reasons, nobody's going to be satisfied with purely a priori attempts to determine who's better off than who.

The idea of measuring happiness for purposes of social policy, however, hasn't pushed us very far towards a clear and consistent answer to the standard philosophical questions about what happiness is (see Chapter 2). Although some thinkers believe that well-being is the focus of social policy, and so hope to be able to determine what it is, others suggest using other concepts instead of it, either because they're more easily measurable, or because well-being isn't suitable for the purposes at hand.

The tendency to think that happiness isn't easily enough measured is illustrated by those economists and other social scientists who think that what ought to be distributed by social or political policy isn't well-being, but *money*. If you think that well-being is too imponderable to be reliably measured and calculated, money seems like a tempting surrogate.

One economist who exemplifies the view that well-being isn't always the most suitable thing for social policy to focus on is Amartya Sen. He's especially concerned with how to measure and compare and assess fairness and unfairness, or distribution. How to do this? Certain obvious measures are clearly inadequate. Money isn't appropriate, because some wealthy people are in an obviously miserable state. Moreover an amount of money isn't always equivalent to a given amount of measurable purchasing power. The fact that we're often concerned to measure purchasing power makes clear that what we really want to measure isn't money *per se*, but something to do with what it can do. But what? Contentment seems ruled out too. Some people are contented who are miserably provided for, and counting them as equally well off with the contented or discontented super-rich builds into one's measurement what Sen takes to be an obvious unfairness.

Sen focuses on what he calls "capabilities" or "capability to achieve valuable functionings." That, he says, is what ought to be distributed justly and fairly (and is relevant to other values as well). In saying this, Sen is cutting loose from the traditional philosopher's notion of happiness. That is, he's cutting loose from an attempt to give an overall evaluation of a person's condition that will take all intuitively relevant aspects of it into account. It doesn't involve itself in the attempt, that is, to answer the question how to assess a person's condition in an all-in way (see Chapter 2). Instead he's looking at a narrower concept: fairness of distribution. There may be no reason for that to coincide with the overall notion of happiness.

One can think of Sen's view as saying this: whatever happiness may be, the important value to focus on for questions of distribution is capabilities, not happiness in any traditional sense. That view can be assessed independently of what one thinks happiness itself might be (or even independently of whether one thinks that there is any such usable concept). That's no criticism of the view. It is certainly arguable that for the purposes that Sen has in mind, it's better to talk not about happiness as traditionally conceived, but about an aspect or part of it (see Chapter 7).

Sen's way of thinking seems to me to typify the efforts to evaluate and quantify the condition of a human being that we usually encounter nowadays. Those efforts pick out and stress a certain aspect or part of what might more broadly be thought of as well-being. Not without good reason either. As I've stressed, integrating the various aspects of happiness and our viewpoints on them isn't easy to do. Moreover it does seem that certain among these aspects are especially pertinent to certain purposes, and not to others. Sen's line of thought (whether or not in the end one accepts it) is understand-able, given his particular purposes.

The phenomenon that we're noticing here is the devaluation of the concept of happiness, and various moves to replace it piecemeal – for particular local purposes of policy and in the social sciences – by other concepts. The social sciences today tend to focus on those other concepts (although there are exceptions; see Kahneman et al. 1999), and aim less than one might expect for an account of the concept of happiness itself. After all, the notion of happiness is in some respects pretty coarse-grained and general. Investigators in the social sciences, however, are often interested in more fine-grained results. They often want to know what quite specific states of mind will lead people to engage in particular forms of activity: to vote for a particular candidate, or purchase a particular product, or adopt certain social attitudes, and so on. For these purposes a generalized examination of happiness may not be very useful. This isn't what one might have expected the legacy of nineteenth-century utilitari-anism to produce, but it seems to be happening.

As long as there's heavy pressure to find unproblematically quan-tifiable measures of these sorts, one can expect this trend to con-tinue. The concept of happiness will give ground to other concepts. If quantitative hedonism can't do what Bentham expected of it, there isn't any obvious alternative explication of happiness that comes close to capturing the ground that it covers. Rather, one should expect to find its role being taken over by concepts of more easily measurable states of people. These will in all probability be closely connected to happiness as it has traditionally been construed, and probably most of them will seem to be aspects of it, not the whole of it (see Chapter 7).

Obstacles to Empiricism about Happiness

At some periods, I've said, there's been a degree of consensus con-cerning some facts about happiness. Furthermore the nineteenth and twentieth centuries have seen an increasing optimism about the capacity of empirical methods to identify and measure at least certain aspects of it. But this tendency has led many people, instead, to adopt other concepts of what's to be measured and distributed, so that the role that happiness once played has been fragmented.

Other developments have led people to doubt that happiness is, after all, an empirical concept, or that ascriptions of happiness can be firmly based on empirical grounds, or indeed on any firm grounds. Do people expect to find a clear syndrome of symptoms to which being happy leads, or a well-defined class of causes of happiness?

One might well doubt it. For one thing, there are many different aims and desires whose satisfaction is involved in happiness. However, those aims generally aren't satisfied together. Moreover, as noted, the satisfactions of them are to some extent incompatible (see Chapter 2). That obviously lessens the chances of finding psychological regularities that say generally, "If a person's happy then he's likely to do such-and-such," or "If such-and-such happens to a person, then he's likely to be happy." What a person does when he's happy, and what will make him happy, are too varied and dependent on the person's beliefs and tastes, etc., and on surrounding circumstances too, for very many straightforward empirical regularities involving happiness to emerge.

In addition, there's also the fact that happiness is variously associated by different people with a multiplicity of conscious states, such as calm contentment, ecstasy, hilarity, elation, and others. These states all have some claim to be parts or aspects of happiness (or to be, more likely, aspects or accompaniments of parts of it). However, they certainly don't all obtain together, and some of them, once again, seem incompatible with each other – ecstasy and calm contentment, for instance. It's difficult to see how the effort to find psychological laws involving happiness might cope with this fact.

In fact it may be that what some philosophers have held is true of terms designating virtues – "brave," "magnanimous," etc. – holds also for "happy." That is, it may be that happiness is one of those concepts of "folk psychology" that doesn't designate any psychological state, and can't have any explication in terms of the kind of science that tries to discover general laws or regularities (see Harman 1999– 2000).

That would be one reason why there hasn't been much pressure for such empirical investigators, with such motivations, to work on the traditional task of determining how the various components of well-being fit together under an all-in concept of well-being. I've emphasized the fact that as we think of happiness, it involves a plurality of aims and the like that can conflict, as assessed from a plurality of sometimes inconsistent standpoints (see Chapter 1). The overall concept of happiness is supposed to take all of these in. The question has been: how? The issues that lead to most empirical studies of what people do, and the concerns that motivate them, haven't generated either much pressure to try to answer that question, nor ways of doing so.

There are in fact serious obstacles, seemingly inherent in the concept itself, in the way of treating it as a clearly specifiable empirical notion. Some of these obstacles have come to light with special clarity in philosophical discussion over the twentieth century. But they're visible in treatments of happiness by ancient philosophers as well. Already in antiquity substantial problems had arisen for the idea that calling someone happy is a straightforward sort of judgment.

Many readers of Aristotle have asked themselves the question whether his account of happiness is "naturalist" in the sense noted above. The idea that it might be one is stimulated by his emphasis on the fact that in order to find out what happiness is, we have to *observe* what people aim at. That might suggest that our ascriptions of happiness are based simply on observations of people's behavior – the same idea that motivates the empiricist thinking of Mill much later. That would mean that as he saw things, his definition of the human good or happiness as "activity of the soul in accordance with excellence, or if there is more than one excellence, with the best and most complete" (*Nicomachean Ethics* 1098a17–18) was established empirically. But if we make that bald statement, we're in danger of attributing to Aristotle a sharper notion of the "empirical" than any that he actually had.

There's reason, however, not to understand him in such a straight-forwardly empiricist way. For one thing, there's the fact that his argument generates conclusions about what a person aims at *as* a human being. It turns out that in his view some people, and indeed many of them, to all appearances *don't* aim at what he says happiness is. They aim at pleasure or fame or something else, because they mistake what the human good is.

So it looks as though something besides straightforward observation is supposed to stand behind his definition and to support it. Things that some people do aim at are being filtered out, on the ground that those people don't, according to Aristotle, aim at those things "*as* human beings." That filtering has the look of being based on a prior evaluative judgment about what human beings *ought* to aim at. So the basis of the definition isn't intended to be observation alone.

Aristotle exhibits the sort of question that can be raised about judging whether someone is happy, i.e. whether it's an empirical matter. Some philosophers, however, clearly think that in principle the task presents no serious difficulty. That's shown by their many unhesitating ascriptions of happiness and its opposite.

On the other hand it does seem to involve difficulties of principle. If you look at happiness as a summing up that takes into consideration all of a person's aims, etc., and whether and to what degree they're fulfilled, there are two kinds of problems.

One problem is this. It's not always a clear-cut issue whether someone has a particular aim or not, or whether a person believes a certain thing to be worthwhile, or enjoys it, etc. When this is so, it will be correspondingly hard to determine someone's well-being. That is, to the extent that constituents of happiness are described by notions that aren't easy to pin down, so that one can tell (for example, after observation) who falls under them, the ascription of happiness will be made problematic. If happiness includes getting something of what you want, and if it's hard to determine what you want, then it will obviously be hard to determine how happy you are.

The other problem is much more difficult. Happiness in the normal sense involves quite a lot of components (even a lot of aims and wants), and it's extremely hard to say, as we've seen (especially in Chapter 2) which of them plays a significant role in happiness and what role they play. To the extent that *that*'s hard to say, it's also going to be hard to say who counts as happy and to what extent. Even if you knew which components were important, it would evidently be problematic to know how much or in what way to count each of them. Furthermore a great deal of disagreement prevails about this issue, as the history of happiness amply testifies.

Moreover, if it's not an empirical question which constituents of happiness play which roles, it can't be an empirical question how happy someone is. That latter question would have to include the former as a non-empirical component. Using purely empirical methods to settle how happy someone is would be out of the question.

This fact notwithstanding, happiness has to some extent been treated as an empirical feature of a person's condition. So it must have at least some significant components that people think of as determinable by observation. Aristotle might be an example of this view. Another one is the Hellenistic idea that happiness is very largely a matter of tranquillity. Moreover, quite a lot of work is being done nowadays by empirical psychologists to try to explore the notion of well-being, "toward the age-old goal of understanding human happiness" (Kahneman et al. 1999). In the concluding chapter I return to the question whether this is a reasonable ambition for investigation.

Chapter 7

Doing without the Concept

Trying to Put the Puzzle Together

If having a concept of happiness requires that it meets a high standard of clarity, then you might well say that we don't really have a concept of happiness, or at least that it certainly doesn't show itself in the history of philosophy.

That idea of the concept of happiness looks as follows. A person has various aims, desires, aspirations, things that he regards as worthwhile, things that he enjoys, and so on. Not knowing how to fit all of these things together into a limited time, or how to see them as compatible with each other, or to be sure which of them he should pursue at all or how much, he asks what it is to be happy. He asks this because he expects the answer to *guide* him in dealing with his various aims, etc. He thinks that it will show him which of them should be retained, and how those that should be retained fit together.

Compare such a person to someone who has a lot of puzzle pieces, but doesn't know what picture they're supposed to make up when they're put together, or even which of them actually belong to the puzzle. He thinks that if he knew the picture he'd be able to determine which pieces belong and how they fit together. The picture will guide him, he thinks, in assembling the pieces.

We might try to use this simile to convey one idea of what it would be like to possess an adequate concept of happiness. A simile like this one influences many philosophical attempts to articulate what happiness is. But our possession of the concept of happiness isn't what this simile suggests.[1]

Philosophers and others expect the concept to provide guidance of this kind. They not infrequently say that the concept of happiness is like the picture on the puzzle, and that it would enable them to put the pieces – the various aims, etc. – together in the, or some, right way. Many philosophers have tried to identify a guiding concept. Bentham and Mill, for instance, claim that by identifying happiness as pleasure – though in different ways – they're helping provide a criterion for right action. Epicurus had said the same thing, although his notion of pleasure had been yet another one. Plato made the same claim for his identification of the best human condition as harmony of the personality. Hobbes and Kant, though, had denied that there's any such guiding concept. Nietzsche seemed to agree that there isn't one, and also asserted that a person's better off if he doesn't have one. These are just some examples.

The existence of long-standing disagreement about how to identify a guiding concept of happiness isn't a demonstration that there's no right way to do it. Furthermore it wouldn't be in place here, in a short history of the issue, to try to mount such a demonstration.

Even so, it makes some sense to try to say, very briefly, why one might well doubt that we have the kind of guiding concept of happiness that philosophers have looked for. It also makes sense to say what kind of alternative there might be. This is especially so in view of the fact that one of the major figures in the history of happiness, Aristotle, can be understood as having proposed an alternative. I'll conclude by presenting this way of construing his thinking. First, though, I'll say more about the difficulties that attempts to find a guiding concept have encountered.

I think that we should be struck by how very little there is to say about what speaks for one identification of happiness over another.

This makes me doubt that we have a single concept of happiness here, and it makes me doubt, too, that we're witnessing various philosophers offering identifications of one and the same concept.

They're all working with the same *problem*. It is and always has been the problem of how to take all of our multiple aims, etc., duly into consideration – in view of the fact that they can't all be fulfilled or even pursued at once – and make of them an overall measure of a person's condition.

However, it would be hard to defend the thesis that beyond *that problem*, they all have a common conception of what a solution to it would be, and that they're all offering an identification of happiness that fits *that* conception. Rather, all they – and we – start with is that problem. The conclusion should be, I'll maintain, that that problem is all that the concept of happiness consists in.

Consider the radically varying ways in which philosophers have approached the question what happiness is. To begin with, in the *Nicomachean Ethics* Aristotle says (to cite it once again) that happiness is "activity of the soul in accordance with excellence, or if there's more than one excellence, in accordance with the best and most complete excellence" (1098a17–18).

Having decided that indeed there is more than one excellence, he then proceeds to determine which of them is the "best and most complete." He concludes that it's excellence at philosophical thinking or "contemplation." He infers that the happiest life is a life devoted to that activity. Thus contemplation turns out to be the dominant end or aim of a happy life.

Compare Epicurus. He maintains that the good is a certain kind of experience, namely pleasure, which he identifies with freedom from disturbance. He recommends living life so that it contains as little disturbance as possible. Bentham said something roughly analogous. He thinks that the good is the experience of pleasure in a more everyday sense, which includes much besides freedom from disturbance. He takes an individual to be happy in proportion to the amount of pleasure his life contains.

Plato has in view both experiences (like Epicurus and Bentham) and activities (like Aristotle). He holds that the best picture shown by the puzzle would be a harmonious arrangement of all kinds of things that are present in a normal life. In an ideal society, he supposes, a harmonious arrangement would be the one that will enable the person to perform his function within that society.

These three philosophers are like three people who approach the task of putting together a puzzle in three very different ways. At first the ways seem to have something in common. Thus the three philosophers might give the impression of working from a common idea of how to solve the puzzle rightly. As one sees what they do, however, this impression is dispelled.

Aristotle is like someone who expects the picture eventually formed by the puzzle to give special prominence to one of its pieces, the best piece. This piece is to have a large and important place, and the others cluster around it.

Epicurus and Bentham, however, want the puzzle to be put together so that the picture contains as little (in the case of Epicurus) or as much (Bentham) of a certain color as possible.

Plato wants the picture to have a coordinated variety of the different designs that are on different pieces, organized for the eye by a particular design: the one on the piece corresponding to reason.

Each puzzle-solver thinks that the best puzzle solution would be the one that most fully exhibits the kind of arrangement that he's concentrated attention on. But now we've lost our grip on the notion of fitting the pieces together that we thought we'd started out with. Or rather, it turns out to amount to different things. It turns out that it doesn't mean what it sounded like, namely, what actually goes on when one works on a puzzle – which is to get the outlines of the pieces to line up snugly with each other. Instead, "fitting" can now mean the physical collocation of the pieces, or the coordination of their colors to highlight or maximize a particular visual feature, or an arrangement that makes the pattern on one of them organize the rest for the eye.

The simile of the puzzle merely suggests to us how these accounts of happiness speak to different concerns. They don't exhibit a concept of happiness that guides a philosopher how to take all of the pieces into consideration in the best way. Not only are different results strived for. Even more significant, different notions of "fitting together" have been brought to bear.[2]

This, I'd say, is what's happened throughout the long series of philosophical attempts to explain what happiness is. We start with the problem of dealing with our various aims. We're aware of local conflicts between particular things that we strive for. We then try to deal with the conflicts in different ways, each of which we take to be appropriate to what we're doing at the time. We then think that we generalize the idea in two ways, to try to form an all-embracing concept of happiness. We suppose that we can take all of our aims into a complete scheme of "coordination"; and at the same time we suppose that the same kind of coordination is applicable across the board. There is, however, no general notion of coordination that's actually used to give us guidance about what to do.

The Concept as the Problem

If we don't adopt the idea that grasping the concept of happiness guides us in dealing with the plurality of sometimes conflicting aims that we have, we can try to apply a different way of thinking about it. This is the notion – a roughly Kantian notion – of a *regulative* ideal or regulative concept. A regulative concept in the relevant sense is a concept that sets before us a certain *task* for our thinking, but without making clear to us how to fulfill it, or even assuring us that in the end it can be fulfilled at all.

In the case of happiness, the task would be to find the right viewpoint from which to combine and organize and sometimes reconcile the various things that we desire and think worthwhile. Entertaining this notion would challenge us to think of an optimal way to organize or combine all of our various aims, etc., and the different viewpoints from which we might do that. But invoking the name "happiness" wouldn't assure us that that can be done, nor *a fortiori* how to do it.

Thinking of the concept of happiness as regulative in this sense is in some ways helpful. If it doesn't guide us in coping with our multiplicity of aims, it suggests that we need to do that. In that sense it's "regulative." On the other hand, it's important to bear in mind just how little regulating the concept of happiness actually does. Not only does it not tell us how to coordinate our aims. It doesn't even tell us what "coordinating" is.

For coordinating doesn't *have* to consist, for instance, in what Plato called "harmonizing." Aristotle rightly rejects the thesis that the more unification there is, the better. Nietzsche presses that rejection further – to an extreme, perhaps, but he does seem to be right that having (in various senses) incompatible aims isn't always a bad thing. Both of them seem to be right that we can't think of the problem as *simply* the minimization of the most familiar kinds of conflict that we experience when we contemplate two incompatible aims immediately before us.

If that's right, then we can't think of the concept of happiness as regulative in any very substantial sense. Trying to grasp it doesn't tell us how to deal with our aims in relation to each other. And it doesn't even tell us much about what "dealing with them in relation to each other" consists in.

The problem associated with the notion of happiness goes deeper than it seems to. Kant's reservations about the notion don't measure its full extent.

Kant bases those reservations on the pervasive uncertainty of our knowledge of the empirical world:

> [I]t is impossible for the most insightful and at the same time most powerful, but nonetheless finite, being to frame here a determinate concept of what it is that he really wills. Does he want riches? How much anxiety, envy, intrigue might he not thereby bring down on his

head? . . . Or long life? Who guarantees that it would not be a long misery? Or health at least? How often has infirmity of the body kept one from excesses into which perfect health would have allowed him to fall, and so on? (*Critique of Practical Reason*, Bk. II, ch. ii)

Kant's conclusion (shortly afterwards in the *Critique*) is a rejection, on the ground of this uncertainty, of the rationality of aiming for happiness:

> In brief, he is not able on any principle to determine with complete certainty what will make him truly happy, because to do so would require omniscience.

We desire one thing, Kant says, but we can't be certain what will happen if we get it. We can't be certain which of our other desires will be satisfied or thwarted.

In particular, Kant is pointing out a certain problem about the coordination of desires. We can't be certain, he notes, what effect the fulfillment of one desire will have on another. If you satisfy your desire for a long life, that may lead to the frustration of another desire, namely the desire not to be in an infirm state.

Kant's diagnosis, however, touches only the surface of the problem that the concept of happiness forces on us. The real problem doesn't arise from our lack of certainty about the course of events in the world. Even if we knew with certainty everything there is to know about the consequences of our aims being realized, that knowledge still wouldn't give us a definite way of evaluating the various possible ways in which the fulfillment of our aims might be combined. We'd still have a large plurality of possible combinations of aims, and a plurality of viewpoints from which to evaluate them comparatively. Therefore we'd still have a plurality of answers to the question, "Which overall situation, with all aims and considerations taken into account, would make me better off?" (see Chapter 2). That's because the problem isn't fundamentally one of empirical predictability. It's one of how to evaluate a whole collection of aims taken somehow together, when one's interest in doing that is initiated mainly just by one's having them as aims separately.

Kant is therefore right that we don't have a clear idea of how our aims, etc., are to be taken into consideration all together. But that's not because we can't make certain predictions about their repercussions for each other. It's because even if we knew all the repercussions, we don't have a determinate way of evaluating the various possible combinations.

Where We Are Again

We might ask whether the concept of happiness has a regulative function, not of telling us how to organize our aims, not of making clear to us what "organizing" consists in, but of *negative* regulation. Perhaps, that is, we should take the guiding content of the concept of happiness as the avoidance of conflict between aims, activities, etc. (somewhat on the model of Epicurus' view that pleasure is the *absence* of something).

Grasping the concept of happiness, then, wouldn't tell us what it is for a set of aims to be dealt with in a good way. It would simply tell us what it is for a set of aims to be unsatisfactory. It would tell us, that is, what we started out knowing, and what Plato started the whole discussion of happiness by pointing out: that our aims conflict, and that that situation needs attention and some remedy. And it would then tell us that we need a way of thinking about how, generally and overall, to avoid such difficulty in our entire collection of aims, etc.

This suggestion, though, misses the point. We don't *need*, or use, a *general* notion of happiness to tell us that in certain cases our aims conflict, and that that's an undesirable state to be in. Similarly we don't need, and don't use, a general notion of "conflict of aims" to tell us in many particular cases that two immediate aims conflict, just as we don't need or use a general notion of "aim" to aim at certain things, or a general notion of "desire" to have an explicit and articulated desire for something.

The view that we don't need a general concept is, I think, an old one. It's fundamentally an Aristotelian view – as I think Aristotle should be interpreted. It's a difficult idea, and cuts against the grain of the tradition – which is chiefly a Platonic one – of supposing that to the extent that we could understand how our plurality of aims might be dealt with, we'd have to do that by appeal to a general conception of overall happiness.

The Platonic view – which informs both Plato's conception of how to evaluate the human condition and also many conceptions that derive historically from it – is to say that when we recognize that it's unsatisfactory to have conflicts and frustrations, we thereby exhibit a grasp – an inexplicit and partial grasp – of what a satisfactory condition would be. By the same token, Plato thinks that when we sense that our aims conflict, we do that by having an idea of the harmony of aims that we can tell isn't exemplified. The reasonable avoidance of conflict and frustration, he infers, is possible only through the clear articulation of the harmony of aims that's lacking. That harmony is happiness.

Not all philosophers have agreed with Plato's identification of happiness with a harmony of aims, let alone the function-based harmony that he describes in the *Republic*. But many of them have tacitly agreed with him that dealing with the negative side of the coin – conflict and frustration of aims – requires defining explicitly what the positive side – happiness – would be like. Many have even agreed with another of his assumptions. That's the assumption that we understand what conflict and frustration of aims are, and what's bad about them, only by grasping what coordination of aims is, and what's good about it.

As a guide to getting us out of conflicts and other problems, Plato recommends a philosophical program of articulating – in a definition or other such account – what harmony is (and, in his scheme in the *Republic*, what the good is). Without this guidance, Plato thinks, we can't improve our condition effectively.

The sense that there must be a way of doing this has remained strong for a long time. It's expressed also by a philosopher as different from Plato as Sidgwick, in his statement that "deeply rooted in the moral consciousness of mankind" is the conviction with regard to practice that "there cannot be really and ultimately any conflict between . . . two kinds of reasonableness." For, Sidgwick thinks, there simply must be a coherent account of an "ultimate good,"

> a final criterion of the comparative value of the different objects of men's enthusiastic pursuit, and of the limits within which each may legitimately engross the attention of mankind. (*The Methods of Ethics*, pp. 405–6)

Sidgwick's conviction that there must be such a final criterion was blocked, for him, by the Dualism of Practical Reason (Chapter 5).

Aristotle, as I've indicated, suggests a different approach, though occasionally, it has to be said, he slips back into a more Platonic way of thinking. Aristotle's own tendency, in the first place, is to think that we can conceive of a satisfactory human condition *without* defining a general idea of the good. He criticizes Plato for trying to use such a general notion for practical guidance (*NE* I.6). In this respect his outlook is similar, surprisingly enough, to the otherwise disparate thinking of Lewis, Sartre, and Bratman, with their emphasis on the openness of human plans, intentions, and self-evaluations (see Chapter 4).

Aristotle tries to show how we can construct a notion of happiness out of what we take – in particular cases or in relatively narrow types of cases – to be the particular aims that we actually have, *not* some general concept of happiness into which those aims are expected to fit. (This strategy almost inevitably, it seems, entails sacrificing the idea of the guidance of a non-actual, unrealized goal; that, in turn, subjects him to the charge of political conservatism, which is largely accurate.) Aristotle tries to take account of the particular aims that (he holds) most people in fact have. He tries to base his account on observation as much as he can (see Chapter 6). His description of happiness, as an overall condition, is supposed – whether he succeeds in this or not – to be derived entirely from the observation of these particular human aims.

Thinking of Aristotle in this light, we should regard his view that consistency in aims is in general to be sought as supported simply by the fact that people *do in fact aim at* consistency. It's not an "external" or a "formal" constraint on the structure of a set of aims, or a prior constraint that people bring to the aims that they have. Rather, what we call "consistency" is one of the aims that people actually have, on a par with the desire for food, the company of other people, and so on.

Neither, in Aristotle's sort of view, is the idea itself of consistency of aims something that one brings to the set of aims that one is presented with. Nor is dealing with those aims achieved by grasping a general notion of what it is for one aim to fit with another within a global happiness.

A general description is, of course, sometimes available to present how various cases of what's called "consistency" can be classified together. However, the comprehension of the fact that you can't both finish your work and watch a movie doesn't depend on, or arise from, a grasp of an inclusive general concept of happiness. Nor, for the most part, does one's decision about which to do, or how much to do of each. Such harmonizings of conflicting ends are understood and done piecemeal in various kinds of situations, in response to needs that are then taken to apply to them.

We should think in the same way about Aristotle's statement concerning the structure of aims early in the *Nicomachean Ethics*:

> If, then, there is some end of the things that we do, which we desire
> for its own sake (everything else being desired for the sake of this),

and if we do not choose everything for the sake of something else (for *at that rate the process could go on to infinity, so that our desire would be empty and vain*), clearly this must be the good and the chief good. (1094a17–22, my emphasis)

The claim implied by the italicized words is that we don't aim at things that way; we do aim at things either for themselves or as parts of a chain leading to some single overall aim.

Aristotle's project thus isn't – as Plato's was and as that of most philosophers has been – to demonstrate a way of harmonizing or coordinating ends. As noted (Chapter 4), Aristotle says that there are two human aims – contemplation and politics – not just one. He also indicates that it's best for any given person to take, if possible, only one of them as his dominant aim. But that's not to say that a full coordinated realization of human aims, severally or collectively, is achieved by doing that. Rather, one of the aims is inevitably sacrificed. That's a loss of value in a person's life, compared with what he still aims at, and it's regarded by him as such.

Aristotle's view thus leaves us for the most part where we were, with our actual attempts – which we all make anyway – to pursue our aims and try to deal with all difficulties in achieving them, regardless of whether those difficulties come from conflicts or other factors. As we develop a picture of what life is to be like, we don't start from a "framework" concept of happiness (an idea of what the picture on the puzzle is to be), to which we tailor our particular aims so that they'll fit into it. Rather, we simply have particular aims: some very specific and some more general or complex or systematic. For the most part, we build up a conception of what happiness would be out of the aims that we have. But we never have or try for a *completely and consistently articulated* concept of happiness, or even suppose that there must be such a thing, or a criterion for it such as was sought by Plato, Sidgwick, and much of the rest of the tradition of work on the concept. If that's right, then in an important sense the history of the concept of happiness has been a search for something that's unobtainable.

Notes

1 Compare Wittgenstein's treatment of related themes in his *Philosophical Investigations*. The following way of reading Aristotle in tandem with Wittgenstein follows some of the same lines suggested by McDowell, "Virtue and reason" (1998).

2 This idea is analogous, partly, to a good point of Sen's, which he puts this way: "What counts as 'consistency' is basically undecidable without taking some note of the motivation of the chooser" (*Rationality and Freedom*, 2002: 20).

Glossary and List of Historical Figures

The numbers in square brackets after entries indicate the chapters of this book containing significant discussion.

Aristippus of Cyrene (c.435–c.355 BC). Roughly contemporary with Plato, a defender of a hedonist view similar to that of "Callicles" in Plato's *Gorgias*. [3, 7]

Aristotle (384–322 BC). Pupil of Plato. In his *Nicomachean Ethics*, the human good is happiness, or well-being, which is "activity of the soul in accordance with excellence or . . . with the best excellence." [1, 3, 4, 5, 6, 7]

Jeremy Bentham (1748–1832). The originator of the ethical theory known as utilitarianism, and of quantitative hedonism. [2, 3, 6]

Michael Bratman (1948–). American philosopher doing research on human action. [7]

Joseph Butler (1692–1752). Moral philosopher, and author of a famous argument against the thesis that "self-love," or the desire for one's own good, is the only human motivation. [2, 3, 6]

George Gordon Byron, sixth baron (1788–1824). Romantic poet. The suitability of the epithet, taken both in an intuitive and in a more special sense, was manifested in both his writings and his life. [2]

"Callicles." A probably fictional character in Plato's dialogue, the *Gorgias*. [2, 3]

"Céline," the pen name of the writer, **Louis-Ferdinand Destouches** (1894–1961). In a characteristically violent way he rejects the idea of foresight and prudence. [2]

Cicero (Marcus Tullius Cicero) (106–43 BC). Roman lawyer, politician, man of letters with an interest in philosophy, and translator of Greek philosophical works into Latin.

Samuel Clarke (1675–1729). A British philosopher with interests mainly in metaphysics and theology, somewhat also in ethics. [5]

The classical period. The period of Greek philosophy and history running from the late fifth century BC until the death of Alexander the Great in 323 or of Aristotle in 322. [3, 6]

Benjamin Constant (1767–1830). Liberal Swiss political thinker, one of the important proponents of the idea of limited government.

Richard Cumberland (1632–1718). British moral philosopher and critic of Hobbes, author of *A Treatise of the Laws of Nature* (1672). [5]

Democritus (mid-fifth to mid-fourth century BC). Atomist physical philosopher (called a "pre-Socratic" although he was born after Socrates and died after him), and apparently an advocate of a kind of hedonism. [2]

René Descartes (1596–1650). Rationalist philosopher and mathematician. [4]

Charles Dickens (1812–70). Nineteenth-century English novelist. Social issues are prominent in his works. [3]

Ralph Waldo Emerson (1803–82). American thinker, representative of the "Transcendentalist" movement. [2]

Empiricism. The view in the theory of knowledge according to which all knowledge derives from sense experience, either by being caused by it or by being justifiable only on the basis of it. [3, 6]

Epicurus (c.340–270 BC). Greek philosopher, founder of the Epicurean school, who espoused a quasi-quantitative form of hedonism. [3]

Philippa Foot (1923–). Twentieth-century British moral philosopher, influenced by Aristotle. [5]

Sigmund Freud (1856–1939). Psychologist and founder of psychoanalysis. [2]

Gorgias. Fifth-century BC rhetorician, Sophist, and philosopher, criticized by Plato in the dialogue named after him. [2, 3]

T. H. Green (1836–82). British idealist philosopher strongly influenced by Hegel. [5]

G. W. F. Hegel (1770–1831). Influential German philosopher and critic of Kant. [5]

Hellenistic period. The period of Greek philosophy and history running roughly from the death of Alexander the Great in 323 BC and Aristotle in 322 into the period of increasing Roman domination of the Mediterranean Sea over the second century BC.

Herodotus (c.484–c.430 BC). Greek writer on matters historical and anthropological, author of a book nowadays called *The Persian Wars*.

Thomas Hobbes (1588–1679). English philosopher and political theorist, author of *Leviathan* and many other works. [2, 3, 5]

David Hume (1711–76). Highly influential Scottish philosopher, who wrote on epistemology, ethics, and many other areas. [3, 4, 5]

Francis Hutcheson (1694–1746). Scottish philosopher, forerunner of Hume in important respects. [5]

Immanuel Kant (1724–1804). German philosopher and moral theorist, who developed a distinctive and controversial notion of the rationality of morality. [4, 5, 7]

Gottfried Wilhelm von Leibniz (1646–1716). Rationalist philosopher and mathematician. [4]

Clarence Irving Lewis (1883–1964). Twentieth-century American pragmatist philosopher. [4, 7]

John Locke (1632–1704). English philosopher and political theorist, who adopted, in his epistemology, a mixture of empiricism and rationalism. [3, 4]

John Stuart Mill (1806–73). Philosopher who defended and developed the utilitarian position originated by Bentham. [3, 6]

John Milton (1608–74). English poet and writer, author of the epic poem, *Paradise Lost*.

Henry More (1614–87). British moral philosopher, one of the Cambridge Platonists. [5]

Friedrich Nietzsche (1844–1900). German philosopher and scholar, who regarded the notions of morality and of happiness skeptically. [2, 4, 5, 7]

Panaetius of Rhodes (c.185–180 to c.110 BC). Stoic philosopher, who was on friendly terms with numerous important Roman politicians. [4]

Giovanni Francesco Pico della Mirandola (1463–94). Italian Renaissance humanist, heavily influenced by Plato and Neoplatonism. [2, 4]

Plato (c.427–347 BC). Pupil of Socrates, and one of the earliest philosophers to treat the notion of happiness systematically. [2–7 *passim*]

Richard Price (1723–91). English moral philosopher. [5]

Rationalism. The view in the theory of knowledge according to which some knowledge, or alternatively all genuine knowledge, is arrived at through reason, not sense experience. [4, 6]

Thomas Reid (1710–96). Scottish philosopher, one of the founders of the "common-sense" school. [5]

Jean-Paul Sartre (1905–80). French Existential philosopher and writer. [4, 7]

Amartya Sen (1933–). Twentieth-century economist and philosopher. [6]

Henry Sidgwick (1838–1900). Utilitarian and theorist of ethics and political economy. The final and now standard edition of his *Methods of Ethics* appeared in 1907. [3, 5, 7]

B. F. Skinner (1904–90). Behaviorist psychologist, who made strong claims for the value of behaviorism for social policy. [6]

Adam Smith (1723–90). Scottish moral philosopher and economist. [3, 4, 5]

Solon of Athens (flourished around 594 BC). Statesman and one of the proverbial "seven wise men of Greece." [1, 2, 4]

The Sophists. A group of teachers, rhetoricians, and intellectuals active in Greece, and mostly in Athens, in the latter part of the fifth century BC. Some thought of Socrates as a Sophist. The term isn't always pejorative, even in Plato.

Herbert Spencer (1820–1903). British philosopher and sociologist, who attempted to apply a variety of evolutionary theory to ethics. [6]

Baruch (Benedict) Spinoza (1632–77). Rationalist philosopher, who treated both ethical and metaphysical issues. [4]

The Stoics. A Greek philosophical school and movement. It began in Athens around 300 BC, and endured through the rest of antiquity. [4, 5]

"Thrasymachus." A probably fictional character in Plato's *Republic* I, who advocates an egoist position and argues that an individual doesn't benefit from being just. [5, 6]

Lorenzo Valla (1407–57). A Renaissance Christian humanist, he adopted a form of hedonism according to which we love God as the producer of the pleasure of heaven. [3]

Bibliography

This list consists of works that are referred to in the text along with others that especially influenced the writing of this book, or that make more of the relevant historical material available to the reader.

Throughout this book I've quoted from translated works in the editions given here, however with some minor changes. As far as possible I've cited extracts by means of systems of reference that apply to all standard editions, rather than using pagination that would require the reader to procure a particular edition.

Annas, Julia (1993) *The Morality of Happiness.* Oxford: Oxford University Press.

Aquinas, Thomas (1948) *Introduction to Saint Thomas Aquinas*, ed. Anton C. Pegis. New York: Modern Library.

—— (1981) *Summa theologica*, trans. Fathers of the English Dominican Province. Westminster, MD: Christian Classics.

Aristotle (1915) *Eudemian Ethics*, trans. J. Solomon. Oxford: Clarendon Press.

—— (1998) *Nicomachean Ethics*, trans. David Ross, rev. J. L. Ackrill and J. O. Urmson. Oxford: Oxford University Press.

Augustine (1998) *The City of God against the Pagans*, trans. R. W. Dyson. Cambridge: Cambridge University Press.

Bentham, Jeremy (1970) *An Introduction to the Principles of Morals and Legislation*, ed. J. H. Burns and H. L. A. Hart. London: Athlone Press.

Brandt, Richard B. (1989) "Fairness to happiness," *Social Theory and Practice* 15/1 (Spring), pp. 33–58.

—— (1992) "Two concepts of utility," in *Morality, Utilitarianism, and Rights* (pp. 158–75). Cambridge: Cambridge University Press.

Bratman, Michael (1987) *Intentions, Plans, and Practical Reason.* Cambridge, MA: Harvard University Press.

Broad, C. D. (1930) *Five Types of Ethical Theory.* London: Kegan Paul, Trench and Trubner.

Butler, Joseph (1964) Sermon XI, in *Fifteen Sermons Preached at the Rolls Chapel and A Dissertation upon the Nature of Virtue,* with introduction and notes by W. R. Matthews. London: Bell.

Byron, George Gordon (1975) *Childe Harold's Pilgrimage* [1812], in *Childe Harold's Pilgrimage and Other Romantic Poems,* ed. John D. Jump. London: Dent.

Céline (Louis Ferdinand Destouches) (1983) *Voyage au bout de la nuit* (*Journey to the End of the Night*), trans. Ralph Manheim. New York: New Directions.

Cicero (Marcus Tullius Cicero) (1961) *De finibus bonorum et malorum* (*On the Boundaries of Good and Bad*), trans. H. Rackham. Cambridge, MA: Harvard University Press.

—— (1961) *De officiis* (*On Duties*), trans. W. Miller. Cambridge, MA: Harvard University Press.

Clarke, Samuel (1978) *The Works of Samuel Clarke.* New York: Garland.

Constant, Benjamin (1988) "The liberty of the ancients compared with that of the moderns" [1816], in *Political Writings,* trans. Biancamaria Fontana. Cambridge: Cambridge University Press.

Cumberland, Richard (1978) *A Treatise of the Laws of Nature* [1727], trans. John Maxwell, facsimile edition. New York: Garland. *De legibus naturae* first published 1672.

Dante Alighieri (1984) *The Divine Comedy: Paradiso,* trans. Allen Mandelbaum. Berkeley and Los Angeles: University of California Press.

Darwall, Stephen (1995) *The British Moralists and the Internal 'Ought': 1640– 1740.* Cambridge: Cambridge University Press.

Descartes, René (1991) *The Philosophical Writings of Descartes,* ed. John Cottingham, Robert Stoothoff, Dugald Murdoch, and Anthony Kenny, vol. III. Cambridge: Cambridge University Press.

Dickens, Charles (1966) *Hard Times* [1854], ed. G. Ford and S. Monod. New York: Norton.

—— (1977) *Bleak House* [1853], ed. G. Ford and S. Monod. New York: Norton.

Diogenes Laertius (1925) *Lives of the Philosophers*, trans. R. D. Hicks, rev. edn. Cambridge, MA: Harvard University Press.

Emerson, Ralph Waldo (1990) "Self-reliance" [1841], in *Essays, First and Second Series*. New York: Vintage.

Ernst, Germana (ed.) (2003) *La filosofia del Rinascimento*. Rome: Carocci.

Foot, Philippa (2001) *Natural Goodness*. Oxford: Clarendon Press.

Freud, Sigmund (2005) *Civilization and its Discontents* (*Unbehagen in der Kultur*, 1930), ed. James Strachey. New York: Norton.

Gibbard, Allan (1986) "Interpersonal comparisons," in Jon Elster and Aanund Hylland (eds.) *Foundations of Social Choice Theory* (pp. 165–93). Cambridge: Cambridge University Press.

Gosling, J. C. B., and C. C. W. Taylor (1982) *The Greeks on Pleasure*. Oxford: Clarendon Press.

Green, T. H. (1907) *Prolegomena to Ethics*, 5th edn. Oxford: Clarendon Press.

Griffin, James (1986) *Well-Being*. Oxford: Oxford University Press.

Haakonsen, Knud (1996) *Natural Law and Moral Philosophy*. Cambridge: Cambridge University Press.

Harman, Gilbert (1999–2000) "The nonexistence of character traits," *Proceedings of the Aristotelian Society* 100, pp. 223–36.

Heap, Shaun Hargreaves, Martin Hollis, Bruce Lyons, Robert Sugden, and Albert Weale (1992) *The Theory of Choice*. Oxford: Blackwell.

Hegel, G. W. F. (1990) *Encyclopedia of the Philosophical Sciences in Outline* [1817], trans. Steven A. Taubenek. New York: Continuum.

Hirschman, Albert O. (1977) *The Passion and the Interests*. Princeton, NJ: Princeton University Press.

Hobbes, Thomas (1994) *Leviathan* [1651], ed. Edwin Curley. Indianapolis and Cambridge, MA: Hackett.

Hollis, Martin, and Robert Sugden (1993) "Rationality in action," *Mind* 102, pp. 1–35.

Hume, David (1978) *A Treatise of Human Nature* [1739–40], ed. L. A. Selby-Bigge, rev. P. Nidditch. Oxford: Clarendon Press.

—— (1985) "Of the standard of taste" [1757], in *Essays Moral, Political, and Literary*. Indianapolis: Liberty Classics.

Hutcheson, Francis (1738) *An Inquiry into the Original of Our Ideas of Beauty and Virtue*. London.

Kahneman, Daniel, and Amos Tversky (eds.) (2000) *Choices, Values, and Frames*. Cambridge: Cambridge University Press.

Kahneman, Daniel, E. Diener, and N. Schwarz (eds.) (1999) *Well-Being: the Foundations of Hedonic Psychology*. Russell Sage Foundation: New York.

Kant, Immanuel (1956) *Critique of Practical Reason*, trans. Lewis White Beck. Indianapolis: Bobbs-Merrill.

—— (1981) *Grounding for the Metaphysics of Morals*, trans. James W. Ellington. Indianapolis: Hackett.

Kent, Bonnie (2003) "The moral life," in A. S. McGrade (ed.) *Cambridge Companion to Medieval Philosophy*. Cambridge: Cambridge University Press.

Leibniz, Gottfried Wilhelm (1969) *Philosophical Papers and Letters*, 2nd edn., ed. L. E. Loemker. Dordrecht: Reidel.

Lewis, Clarence Irving (1946) *Analysis of Knowledge and Valuation*. LaSalle, IL: Open Court.

Locke, John (1693) *A Common-place Book to the Holy Bible*, quoted in Stephen Darwall (1995) *The British Moralists and the Internal 'Ought': 1640–1740*. Cambridge: Cambridge University Press.

—— (1975) *An Essay Concerning Human Understanding*, ed. and with introduction by Peter H. Nidditch. Oxford: Clarendon Press.

Lucretius (1975) *De rerum natura* (*On the Nature of Things*), trans. W. H. D. Rouse, rev. M. F. Smith. Cambridge, MA: Harvard University Press.

Mauzi, Robert (1969) *L'Idée du bonheur dans la littérature et la pensée françaises au xviiie siècle*, 5th edn. Paris: Librairie Armand Colin.

McDowell, John (1998) "Virtue and reason," in *Mind, Value, and Reality* (pp. 50–73). Cambridge, MA: Harvard University Press.

Milton, John (1962) *Paradise Lost* [1667], ed. M. Y. Hughes. Indianapolis: Bobbs-Merrill.

More, Henry (1969) *Philosophical Writings of Henry More*, ed. Flora Isabel MacKinnon. New York: AMS Press.

Nagel, Thomas (1997) *The Last Word*. Oxford: Clarendon Press.

Nietzsche, Friedrich (1966) *Beyond Good and Evil*, in *Basic Writings of Nietzsche*, trans. and ed. Walter Kaufmann. New York: Random House.

Pico della Mirandola, Giovanni (1956) *Oration on the Dignity of Man*, trans. R. Caponigri. Chicago: Gateway.

Reid, Thomas (1969) *Essays on the Active Powers of Man* [1788]. Cambridge, MA: MIT Press.

Reiner, Hans (1974) *Die Grundlagen der Sittlichkeit*. Meisenheim: Hain.

Sartre, Jean-Paul (1956) "Existentialism is a humanism" ("L'Existentialisme est un humanisme"), trans. Walter Kaufmann, in Walter Kaufmann (ed.)

Existentialism: from Dostoevsky to Sartre (pp. 345–68). Cleveland: World Publishers.

Schiller, Friedrich (1967) *Letters on the Aesthetic Education of Man*, trans. Elizabeth M. Wilkinson and L. A. Willoughby, a translation of Schiller's revised edition of 1801. Oxford: Clarendon Press.

Schneewind, Jerome B. (1990) *Moral Philosophy from Montaigne to Kant: an Anthology*, 2 vols. Cambridge: Cambridge University Press.

—— (1998) *The Invention of Autonomy: a History of Modern Moral Philosophy*. Cambridge: Cambridge University Press.

Seabright, Paul (2004) *The Company of Strangers: a Natural History of Economic Life*. Princeton, NJ: Princeton University Press.

Selby-Bigge, L. A. (ed.) (1965) *British Moralists: Being Selections from Writers Principally of the Eighteenth Century*. New York: Dover.

Sen, Amartya (1992) *Inequality Reexamined*. Oxford: Clarendon Press.

—— (2002) *Rationality and Freedom* (esp. chs 1–3, 20–1). Cambridge, MA: Harvard University Press.

Shaftesbury, Anthony Ashley Cooper, Third Earl (1999) *Characteristics of Men, Manners, Opinions, Times, etc.* (including *Inquiry Concerning Virtue or Merit*) [1711], ed. Lawrence E. Klein. Cambridge: Cambridge University Press.

Sidgwick, Henry (1907) *The Methods of Ethics*, 7th edn. London: Macmillan.

—— (1931) *Outlines of the History of Ethics*, 6th edn. Boston: Beacon Press.

Skinner, B. F. (1976) *Walden Two* [1948]. Englewood Cliffs, NJ: Prentice-Hall.

Solon (1999) in *Greek Elegiac Poetry from the Seventh to the Fifth Centuries BC*, ed. and trans. Douglas E. Gerber. Cambridge, MA: Harvard University Press.

Spencer, Herbert (1969) *Social Statics; or The Conditions Essential to Human Happiness Specified, and the First of them Developed* [1865]. New York: A. M. Kelley.

Spinoza, Benedict (1955) "On the improvement of the understanding" [1677], in *Chief Works*, trans. R. H. M. Elwes. New York: Dover.

—— (2000) *Ethics* [1677], trans. G. H. R. Parkinson. Oxford: Oxford University Press.

Stocker, Michael (1990) *Plural and Conflicting Values*. Oxford: Oxford University Press.

Troyer, John (ed.) (2003) *The Classical Utilitarians: Bentham and Mill*. Indianapolis and Cambridge, MA: Hackett.

Urmson, J. O. (1973) "Aristotle's doctrine of the mean," *American Philosophical Quarterly* 10, pp. 223–30.

White, Nicholas (2002) *Individual and Conflict in Greek Ethics*. Oxford: Clarendon Press.

Xenophon (1923) *Memorabilia* (*Memoirs of Socrates*), trans. E. C. Marchant. Cambridge, MA: Harvard University Press.

Index

happiness (*eudaimonia*) (*cont'd*)
  assembling the pieces of the
    puzzle, 162–6
  challenges to, 36–40
  concept, 1–2, 20
  determining, 160–1
  devaluation of concept, 157
  developments since antiquity,
    97–107
  discovering, 142–3
  doubts concerning, 164
  as a fact, 142
  framework for, 173
  indefinite concept of, 134–5
  and need for general concept,
    169–70, 172–3
  plural/conflicting aims, 3–4
  rational vs. incoherent, 36–40
harmony, 78, 102, 165, 167, 170–1,
    172–3
  achieving, 32–6
  and change, 21–4
  criticism of, 88
  desirability of, 84–6, 89
  lack of, 84
  Nietzschean hostility towards,
    28–9
  Platonic, 19–21, 81–8
  rejection of premise, 24–32
  as undesirable, 38
hedonism, 146, 148
  advantages of, 53–4
  and Plato, 45–6, 47–9
  psychological, 51
  rational, 51
  see also quantitative hedonism
Hegel, G. W. F., 109–10, 121–2,
    138–9, 177

Hellenistic period, 144–7, 148, 149,
    177
Herodotus, 126, 177
Hobbes, Thomas, 8, 14, 45–6, 163,
    178
human being
  double nature of, 25
  weak, 28
human nature, 118
Hume, David, 178
Husserl, Edmund, 111
Hutcheson, Francis, 59, 129–30,
    178

inclusivist position, 138–40
indifference, 93, 95–6
interest, 105
interpersonal comparisons of
    utility, 65–7

joy, 101
Judgment Day analogy, 18, 40
judgments, 33–4
justice, 16, 150, 155

Kant, Immanuel, 178
  Critique of Practical Reason,
    107–8, 134
  *Grounding for the Metaphysics of
    Morals*, 107, 132, 134
  and happiness, 14, 107–9, 133–5
  and idea of guiding concept, 163
  and knowledge of empirical
    world, 167–9
  and moral condition/degree of
    happiness, 37, 38–9, 116
  and moral obligation, 119, 121
  reactions to, 137–40